YORKSHIRE TERRIER

SANDY BERGSTROM MESMER

Yorkshire Terrier

Editor: Stephanie Fornino
Indexer: Dianne L. Schneider
Designer: Mary Ann Kahn

TFH Publications®
President/CEO: Glen S. Axelrod
Executive Vice President: Mark E. Johnson
Publisher: Christopher T. Reggio
Production Manager: Kathy Bontz

TFH Publications, Inc.®
One TFH Plaza
Third and Union Avenues
Neptune City, NJ 07753

Discovery Communications, Inc. Book Development Team: Marjorie Kaplan, President and General Manager, Animal Planet Media / Kelly Day, EVP and General Manager, Discovery Commerce / Elizabeth Bakacs, Vice President, Licensing and Creative / JP Stoops, Director, Licensing / Bridget Stoyko, Associate Art Director

©2011 Discovery Communications, LLC. Animal Planet™ and the Animal Planet logo are trademarks of Discovery Communications, LLC, used under license. All rights reserved. *animalplanet.com*

Printed and bound in China

11 12 13 14 15 16   1 3 5 7 9 8 6 4 2

Library of Congress Cataloging-in-Publication Data
Yorkshire terrier / Sandy Bergstrom Mesmer.
    p. cm.
  Includes index.
  ISBN 978-0-7938-3720-5 (alk. paper)
  1. Yorkshire terrier. I. Title.
  SF429.Y6M47 2011
  636.76--dc22

                    2010052560

This book has been published with the intent to provide accurate and authoritative information in regard to the subject matter within. While every reasonable precaution has been taken in preparation of this book, the author and publisher expressly disclaim responsibility for any errors, omissions, or adverse effects arising from the use or application of the information contained herein. The techniques and suggestions are used at the reader's discretion and are not to be considered a substitute for veterinary care. If you suspect a medical problem consult your veterinarian.

Note: In the interest of concise writing, "he" is used when referring to puppies and dogs unless the text is specifically referring to females or males. "She" is used when referring to people. However, the information contained herein is equally applicable to both sexes.

The Leader In Responsible Animal Care for Over 50 Years!®
www.tfh.com

CONTENTS

ORIGINS OF YOUR
YORKSHIRE TERRIER

The Yorkshire Terrier is a bright-eyed, mischievous sprite of a dog.

S hiny and beautiful, bright eyed and cocky, the Yorkshire Terrier looks on the world as his oyster. He is much more confident than his size gives him any right to be. How can this have occurred? A look at his origins may help provide the answer.

THE DEVELOPMENT OF THE DOG

Dogs developed from wolves. Based on many studies and a large number of skull measurements and examinations of the size and structure of the brain, blood, and numbers of chromosomes, all dogs are descended solely from the wolf. Genetically speaking, a wolf is little more distant from the domestic dog than a wild mustang is from a quarter horse.

Some studies suggest that wolves were first domesticated in China about 15,000 years ago. It's logical that wolves initially discovered that humans had delectable garbage dumps and got in the habit of hanging out for easy meals. Over many generations, they became more dependent on their human providers, making the switch from associates to partners and finally to pets. It's easy to look at a Siberian Husky or German Shepherd and think of wolf ancestors, but what about a Yorkshire Terrier? How can a 50- to 100-pound (22.5- to 45.5-kg) creature have anything at all to do with the small and feisty Yorkie? Genetics tells the tale, of course, but there is more to this than just rough facts.

From the beginning, humans and wolves had a synergistic relationship. Wolves helped humans protect their caves and eventually houses, while humans could help the wolves maintain a regular food supply.

An initial change from wolf to dog points firmly to the path the Yorkie would eventually take:

- The smaller wolves needed the humans more than the big ones did.
- The smaller wolves had cuter babies—in other words, the "awwww" factor started right at the beginning of domestication.

So as dogs moved away from being wolves (*Canis lupus*) to dogs (*Canis familiaris*), they became smaller. Small dogs first appeared in the Middle East, and archeological evidence points to the fact that it was here that dogs moved from being humankind's associate to humankind's best friend.

YORKIE BEGINNINGS

Although it may seem to some that the Yorkshire Terrier sprang ready-made to life, he was in fact developed from the clever weaving of several now-extinct breeds in the late 18th and the 19th centuries. The origins of these breeds, and therefore the Yorkie as well, go back much further than that.

The Yorkie is descended from several now-extinct breeds from the late 18th and the 19th centuries.

Many hundreds of years ago, most people in England were tied to the land. They were not allowed to hunt or to keep most hunting dogs. As far back as the Canons of Canute (named after an English king who died in 1035; he set up many laws, or "canons"), these common people, or serfs, were allowed "the little dogs" because "it stands to reason that there is no danger in them." The foresters had a hoop and only the dogs who could pass through its 7-inch (18-cm) diameter could be kept. The little dogs kept home and hearth free of rats and other vermin, as well as providing an occasional rabbit for the pot. They were bred generation after generation to be fearless and independent hunters. Because their owners were bound to the land, prohibited from moving away by a system that demanded not only lifelong servitude to a distant master but also that their children and children's children do the same, their dogs did not move around much either. Thus gene pools were kept small, with neighborhood dogs breeding together.

So it began. Each region had its own variety of little dog, but all needed to be quick-thinking and independent because their hardworking owners did not have the time to cosset them. They also needed to be loyal—their owners wanted dogs who protected the meager family interests—and cheerful. The common people lived lives filled with hard knocks, so they needed dogs who were sprightly and optimistic.

The Waterside (top), Paisley (middle), and Clydesdale (bottom) Terriers all contributed to the development of the Yorkshire Terrier.

Although some conjecture is inevitable, original accounts exist to cover the broad strokes of how Yorkshire Terriers seemingly came "from nowhere" to exist as the unique and distinctive breed they are today. Three breeds—all extinct today—each contributed its unique characteristics: the Waterside, Clydesdale, and Paisley Terriers.

THE WATERSIDE TERRIER

By the time of William IV (born 1765, reigned 1830–1837), the Waterside Terrier, sometimes blue and tan in color, was common in Yorkshire. Slightly longer than tall, with a level topline and an erect or semi-erect ear, he resembled a Welsh Terrier but was much smaller, between 5 and 10 pounds (2 and 4.5 kg). Prized for his loyalty and independent hunting abilities, he was "broken coated," which means that he had a medium-length coat similar to today's Cairn Terrier.

SBM 2010

Watersides emigrated with their owners to Tasmania in Australia, where settlers prized the small blue-and-tan dogs for their ability to detect strangers approaching from great distances.

THE CLYDESDALE AND PAISLEY TERRIERS

The Skye Terrier was a unique breed as early as the 1500s. Sweeping long low bodies and swishing coats behind milady through the dank stone corridors of British castles, Skyes were a favorite of the nobility, even the ill-fated Mary Queen of Scots. But they were also true terriers, fiercely loyal and independent hunters, with courage unmatched in dogdom. They had a hard, nylon-like coat with a definite undercoat.

In the late 18th century, several Skye breeders tried to miniaturize their breed, but the purists of the day won out. No way could these smaller dogs be called Skyes. Denied recognition by the parent club, the "mini-Skyes" were called Paisleys or Clydesdale Terriers, named presumably after those valleys in Scotland. They resembled Skyes, being long and low, but instead of the bigger dog's vigorous 40- to 50-pound (18- to 22.5-kg) proportions, were about 15 pounds (7 kg). They also featured a much softer and finer coat than the Skye's and had the gloss factor that makes a Yorkshire's coat reflective like blue burnished steel. The Paisley was blue and self-colored, which means one single color, while the Clydesdale had what writers of the day called a "linty" coat—tan or flaxen furnishings together with a blue body coat.

The Skye Terrier, ancestor of the Yorkshire Terrier, was a fiercely loyal and independent hunter.

WHAT DOES ALL THIS MEAN?

In short, the Yorkshire Terrier of today is the product of three elements: the blue-and-tan, broken-coated, slightly-longer-than-tall Waterside Terrier; the short-legged, blue, long-coated, glossy Paisley Terrier; and the identical Clydesdale

Terrier with golden-tan, "linty" furnishings. Unique elements came from all three breeds, but they had one thing in common—they were all independent, cheerful, feisty, and loyal.

THE INDUSTRIAL REVOLUTION

Another event in the creation of the Yorkshire Terrier occurred in the late 18th century—the Industrial Revolution, which began in northern England. The newly established factories and foundries quickly developed an insatiable appetite for workers. Scottish weavers and other workers flocked south, bringing along their families, and of course, their dogs.

The workers, streaming out from their backbreaking and monotonous jobs, longed for a pint and a "tickle" at the end of the day and a wager on something, anything to take them away from their drab surroundings. A favorite event was

The hands that began the creation of the elegant dog we know today as the Yorkshire Terrier were working class.

wagering on how long it would take for a big dog to bring down a bull or a bear. But bearbaiting and bullbaiting were outlawed in 1825. So now what? The publicans were desperate for something new to entice customers.

Eureka! A small dog was thrown into a pit with 30 or 40 rats. It wasn't a matter of whether dog or rat would win—it was a matter of how fast the dog could dispatch all of the rodents. The smaller the dog, the more audacious the contest and the better the betting. Favorite breeds must have been the scrappy and tenacious Paisleys, Clydesdales, and Watersides.

The publicans, in their search for ever smaller, ever hardier dogs, liberally mixed the three breeds together. So the hands that began the creation of the elegant sprite we know today as the Yorkshire Terrier were gnarled and working class. They bred the dogs small to earn more money, and they bred them tough as nails.

THE INFLUENCE OF HUDDERSFIELD BEN

The father of the Yorkshire Terrier was a dog named Huddersfield Ben, born in 1865. He was owned by Mrs. Jonas Foster, who set the early fashion in Yorkies, and she entered him in a number of dog shows, many of which he won. Some of Mrs. Foster's big winners after Ben were Bradford Hero and Ch. Ted, who weighed 5 pounds (2.5 kg) and stood 9 inches (23 cm) at the shoulder. Both stud dogs were sires or grandsires of early American imports.

In the mid-1880s, the breed was referred to as the Broken-Haired Scottish Terrier. Weighing between 12 and 14 pounds (5.5 and 6.5 kg), this ratter had his name changed to Yorkshire Terrier by England's Kennel Club.

Thus a new "fancy" terrier was born, and the Victorians fell in love. London pet shops sold small patent leather booties for the small Yorkie paws. Everyone wanted a Yorkshire Terrier peeking out the back of their carriage. These dogs' pewter blue and rich golden tan coats were, indeed, stunning. But underneath the shimmering hair lay the confident gaze of a small working terrier, sure that tomorrow would bring more excitement, and if lucky, a good hunt.

THE YORKSHIRE TERRIER IN THE US

It didn't take long for Americans to notice the beautiful new terrier on the other side of the pond. Yorkshire Terriers were among the first 25 breeds to be recognized by the American Kennel Club (AKC) in 1878. The first AKC Yorkshire Terrier champion of record was P.H. Coombs's Ch. Bradford Harry, who was closely related to Huddersfield Ben. Mr. Coombs was not only a breeder and exhibitor but also a judge and authority on the breed, and he was the first to bring the Yorkshire Terrier into the limelight of the American show scene.

Yorkies dipped in popularity before World War II; as a matter of fact, in the 1940s small dog AKC registrations dipped to 18 percent. A 4-pound (2-kg) morsel named Smokey is credited with repopularizing the breed, reminding the American public that although the Yorkshire Terrier was a miniature dog, he, or perhaps better said, she, could be a mighty one.

FAMOUS YORKIES AND YORKIE OWNERS

Bill Wynne, of the 26th Photo Reconnaissance of the Fifth Air Force, found Smokey when she crawled out of a foxhole in New Guinea. She was adopted by Bill's unit and became a wonderful morale booster. Then a communications line had to be laid under a runway in the Philippines. Rather than tear up the field and expose themselves to the enemy, the unit's members let Smokey come to the rescue—she had the line attached to her collar and crawled though a 70-foot-long (22-m) 8-inch (20.5-cm) culvert to the enthusiastic encouragement of her Bill. After the war, Bill and Smokey returned to Ohio, where they performed at nightclubs, hospitals, and dog shows.

No discussion of the turnaround of the Yorkie's popularity can be mentioned without talking about Goldie Stone. Goldie saw her first Yorkie, Mike, in 1908 at a vaudeville show where she and the dog were performing. Fast-forward 18 years

Yorkshires were among the first 25 breeds to be recognized by the American Kennel Club (AKC).

and Goldie began her Petit line of Yorkshire Terriers with the purchase of the future Ch. Petit Byngo Boy, who was a top winner in the 1930s. Stone's Ch. Petit Magnificent Prince was the first American-bred Yorkshire Terrier to win Best in Show, in 1954.

Yorkie owners know that the Yorkshire Terrier is unparalleled as a cheerful and cheeky buddy. Some famous Yorkie owners have been the fashionable Gisele Bündchen, Joan Rivers, Ivana Trump, Mariah Carey, and Missy Elliott. You could be excused in thinking that these famous women may have sometimes used their animals as an elegant fashion accessory. But singer Justin Timberlake, football great Brett Favre, and actor Bruce Willis—who have all owned Yorkies—would laugh at the idea of "arm candy." Yorkshire Terriers are much more than just a pretty face!

THE YORKSHIRE TERRIER TODAY

Several American Yorkshire Terrier breed clubs came and went over the years, starting with the Yorkshire Terrier Club of America in 1912. None survived until the present Yorkshire Terrier Club of America (YTCA), founded in 1951.

Yorkshire Terriers were the second most popular breed in the AKC in 2007 and 2008. In 2009, the most recent year for which information is available, they were the third most popular. Yes, the breed is lovely and its diminutive size greatly enhances the cuteness factor. But now you know that's not all there is to it!

CHARACTERISTICS
OF YOUR
YORKSHIRE TERRIER

Although Yorkies regularly attract attention through their stunning good looks and diminutive size, they keep the loyalty of their owners with their sparkling personalities. What makes a Yorkie a Yorkie? He comes by his cheeky attitude and stunning good looks through hundreds of years of genetic blending. The mix originated with the blue-and-tan rough-coated Waterside Terrier. Then the silky Paisleys and Clydesdales were added. Mixed well, it was discovered that some of these resultant dogs produced tiny, feisty creatures with flowing, steel-blue coats and a long tan headpiece. Carefully bred together, these dogs eventually bred "true," meaning that over time, the parents produced puppies resembling themselves, who in turn produced similar puppies as well.

PHYSICAL CHARACTERISTICS

A Yorkie is much more than just a pretty face. However, just as in any other breed, the standard of a Yorkshire—that is to say, the list of characteristics that make a Yorkshire a Yorkshire—really does matter.

A standard is a summary of the ideal attributes of a particular breed of dog. There are certain basic things one expects. Then the closer the dog adheres to those traits, the better his quality. No dog will ever be perfect. All will have faults; some more, some less, and these faults in no way affect a dog's ability to be a great pet.

In answer to the question "My Yorkie's ears look wrong. Does that mean he's not purebred?" you can answer in one of two ways:

1. He is purebred but has some discrepancies from the standard.
2. He really isn't a purebred dog. You can go online to get a DNA test. That's the only way to know for sure.

GENERAL APPEARANCE

The overall picture of a Yorkshire is of a small long-coated blue-and-tan dog. His long, straight hair is parted down the middle, from the tip of his nose, then from the back of his head to the top of his tail. A Yorkshire in full show coat is indeed a sight to behold. He glides around the ring effortlessly and looks as if he's floating on air. The Yorkie is compact in construction and carries his head high in an abundance of self-importance.

The Yorkie comes by his cheeky attitude and stunning good looks through hundreds of years of genetic blending.

The overall picture of a Yorkshire Terrier is of a small long-coated blue-and-tan dog.

BODY TYPE: A BIG DOG IN A SMALL PACKAGE

Yorkshire Terriers are square and compact in size. They are rather short backed, and their topline is level. They carry the head high, as they are quite sure that if they are not paying attention they might miss something. The breed is an elegant but mighty mite: a big dog in a small package. Yorkies have no concept of their size and regularly act as though they are many times their actual weight.

SIZE: TINY IS NOT BETTER

In discussing the Yorkshire Terrier standard, it is important to start with their size. The standards of the American Kennel Club (AKC) and Fédération Cynologique Internationale (FCI), an international organization of kennel clubs, ask for a dog who is no greater than 7 pounds (3 kg). Most show dogs are at the top of their standard, and the majority of healthy Yorkies are at least 4 pounds (2 kg). Some pets can be 8 or even 10 pounds (3.5 or 4.5 kg). The 7 pounds (3 kg) asked for in the standard translates to a dog who is about 8 inches (20 cm) at the shoulder. There is no discussion in any standard of "mini" or "teacup" Yorkies, and quality Yorkshire Terrier breeders do not strive for a tiny-sized (under 4-pound [2-kg]) dog. Although the Yorkshire Terrier is indeed one of the smallest dog breeds, it is very important to note that smaller Yorkies are often less healthy and shorter lived than their sturdier counterparts. Smaller may be a curiosity, but it is not better.

THE YORKIE'S HEAD (AND SHOULDERS, KNEES, AND TOES)

A Yorkie's cute head is a primary source of that "aww" factor—his muzzle is quite small in relation to his flat back skull. He has a pronounced stop, or the part of the skull between the eyes that's indented. His ears are small, V-shaped, carried erect, and not too far apart. He has medium-sized round eyes; they are dark chocolate, liquid, and full of intelligence—sometimes too much intelligence. Yorkies can easily figure out how to get the goodie or toy, and they also enjoy training their owners to get the goodie for them. To successfully navigate life with a smarty-pants Yorkie, it's important his owner be at least as smart as he is.

Yorkies come from small terriers with the modified dwarf gene, so his legs are relatively short. But his front and rear legs are straight, with a moderate bend of stifle. His feet are round, with black toenails. He has a medium docked tail, which he carries just above back level. A Yorkie has a proud, free movement matched to his moderate angles. In a full show coat, it looks as though he is floating.

COAT: THE YORKIE'S CROWNING GLORY

Straight and hanging down past his feet, from a part running from the back of his head to the top of his tail, the Yorkshire's coat is his glory. The ideal Yorkshire coat drags on the floor. The coat is silky and glossy in texture, but what does glossy really mean? It means that the coat actually reflects light. When you think of the silk of a Yorkie's coat, don't consider washable silk blouses. Think of your grandmother's glossy, heavy silk curtains, so reflective of light that they almost mirror the room. A great Yorkshire coat is so highly reflective that you can almost get a tan.

When fully mature, the Yorkie's headfall can also ripple down to the ground. The color is a rich

The Yorkshire's beautiful silky coat is his crowning glory.

tan, deeper on the side of the head and the back of the ears and lighter on his feet and the back of his tail.

The Puppy Clip

Most Yorkies who are not currently being shown carry a more practical, feet-showing trim. Other Yorkies feature a puppy clip. This clip takes the coat down to about 1 inch (2.5 cm) or so all over the body. It is easy to care for and practical but changes the look of the dog. Yorkies in a puppy clip look like shaggy blue and tan fuzz balls. The clip is cute in its own way but quite different from the full-coated look!

Hypoallergenic Qualities

No dog with hair is absolutely hypoallergenic. But people who are allergic to dogs are not allergic to their hair but to their dander, which is a combination of hair, undercoat, and skin particles. Basically someone looking for a "hypoallergenic dog" should be looking for a "low-shedding" dog. The more undercoat a breed has, the more it will shed and the less hypoallergenic it will be.

A Yorkshire Terrier has very little undercoat and sheds very little, so he has extremely little dander. He loses his coat at about the same rate a human loses hair. (Your Yorkie requires regular trimming because otherwise his hair will just keep on growing.) Yorkies are considered a good breed for someone who is usually allergic to dogs.

To determine whether your Yorkie puppy is going to be okay with your allergic family member, bring that person along to see the puppies and play with some adult dogs too. If the family member doesn't start sneezing at the breeder's house, she will probably be okay with the new puppy in your home.

PUPPY POINTER

Yorkie puppies are born short-coated and black, with tan points on the muzzle, above the eyes, around the legs, feet, and toes, the inside of the ears, and the underside of the tail. Occasionally Yorkies are born with a white "star" on the chest or on one or more toes. They resemble miniature Rottweilers. It can be quite surprising! By 12 weeks they are still black and tan, but the coat has grown out to the fluff ball stage and they no longer resemble their big cousins.

As the Yorkie ages, his coat grows and on the same hair shaft as the black will appear his ultimate color. A clear tan will slowly replace the black on his head. Most Yorkshires will be their adult shades by the age of 18 months, but a full, regal, floor-sweeping coat can take three or more years to achieve.

COLOR: ONLY HIS HAIRDRESSER KNOWS FOR SURE—BUT DOES SHE?

The color of the Yorkshire's body coat has long been discussed and argued about. It is, in essence, a deep blue-gray. Consider a fine-steel bowie knife with its highly reflective bluish sheen—that's the color of a Yorkshire Terrier coat. Then the headpiece, front of the body, and legs up to the elbows are tan. Not as rich as cream or an Irish Setter brown, the tans in a Yorkshire best resemble the color of a candle's flame and can range from a deep cream on the top of the head to almost a russet on the muzzle and feet. A Yorkshire with correct body and head color is so striking that your friends can be excused in thinking that he has been to an expert colorist at your favorite hair salon. But the Yorkshire Terrier comes by these colors naturally.

Where does the Yorkie exhibit blue exactly, and where are the tans? Basically, the tans are on the head, down the legs, and up the back of the tail. The back is blue. It's in a similar pattern to a Doberman Pinscher, except a Yorkie's "blue" is a genetic dilute of black.

LIVING WITH A YORKSHIRE TERRIER

Some people are outgoing and others are wallflowers. In the same way, different Yorkies have different personalities. But they all carry within them the hardwired personality of their breed: a loyal but independent terrier. The joke around the Internet goes: How many Yorkshire Terriers does it take to change a lightbulb? The answer: just one, but he'll do it if—and when—he feels like it.

The Yorkshire is not a breed that tolerates being dominated by his owners. He likes to live in partnership with them. He is smart—almost too smart—and requires a loving but firm owner who can stay one step ahead of him.

COMPANIONABILITY

Dogs such as Beagles or Cocker Spaniels were bred to work in companionship with other dogs. Not so the Yorkshire. His heritage is that of an independent hunter, a dog who the family let out the door in the morning and welcomed back inside at night. During the day he was expected to keep hearth and home free of vermin without human intervention. For this reason, a Yorkshire is usually very loyal to his own people but can be suspicious and reserved with strangers. He enjoys nothing more than hanging out with his family, willing to be petted and taking treats and goodies as only his due. He is, after all, a Yorkshire!

With Children

Yorkies can get along with children, but they occasionally need to be reminded by their owners that while the kids can smell like puppies and can gyrate like a mouse on the run, they are neither and must be treated with the respect they

Yorkies like living in partnership with their human guardians.

BE AWARE!

It can be easy to think that because the Yorkie is a small dog, he doesn't need to be trained. This is simply not true. Every positive attribute of a Yorkie can have its negative side if not controlled. For example, Yorkies are loyal and protective of their homes. But letting your dog growl and snap at visitors is never acceptable behavior. Yorkies are also excellent problem solvers. But ignored and left too much to their own devices, they will possibly "solve" this boredom by redecorating the house or practicing doggy opera in the backyard. In addition, if untrained, your Yorkie's independence could become stubbornness.

Yorkies actually enjoy being trained; they are smart and value the human companionship that training offers. Yorkies definitely need to know that the rules are firm, but they fare best if taught with rewards rather than heavy punishment. Beware: If you try to rigorously force your Yorkie into submission, you will most likely only succeed in teaching him that you are not worthy as his owner—and friend.

deserve. Yorkies are so cute and small that young children often think of them as stuffed animals and try to treat them that way. This is why children as well as your Yorkie require a thorough understanding of their roles.

Often young children don't know their own strength and can literally suffocate a Yorkie with hugs. For this reason, many responsible breeders will not sell a Yorkshire puppy to a family with children under the age of five. But adult Yorkies, being excellent problem solvers, can sometimes do well with even small children as long as their human parents supervise rigorously and give the Yorkie a breather if he needs it.

Even when you train your own children thoroughly in how to deal with your sometimes squirmy little dog—what about your kids' friends? Any child guest in your house should only hold the dog on the floor. Have the child sit down and then pass your Yorkie to her. If the guest is then distracted or the dog suddenly decides to take off, he won't fall far. And if your dog seems less than thrilled to sit in a strange child's lap, respect his wishes and remove him. That way unhappy accidents can be prevented.

With Other Dogs

The Yorkshire can usually tolerate other dogs, and some get along quite well—in their own fashion. Coming from independent hunting stock, Yorkies often don't like to have other dogs on their turf. The best mix is a female and male together— males often strut and posture at each other, and females often tease and annoy other females, with bad results. But a male Yorkie can be quite protective of a female, even with both being spayed/neutered, and a female will generally accept and tolerate a male around her— especially if he pays proper respect!

Yorkies can even get along with big dogs in some circumstances. One Yorkie I know, Jo Jo, lives with a Rottweiler. (Of course Jo Jo rules the roost.) But this is not always the case. Ask your breeder if you are worried that a potential Yorkie may not be the right fit for your large-dog home. In this area more than any other, your Yorkie needs a loving but firm owner who can tell the difference between enthusiastic play and wild-eyed hectic posturing about to spin out of control. Care must be taken, as the big dog needs to tolerate your small but very large-talking Yorkie.

With Other Pets

Anything that acts like prey—such as mice, rats, and lizards—attract the Yorkshire's hunting skills. Keep such small pets safely in their cages. Even the daintiest Yorkie can watch such creatures with a cat-like intensity, obviously

thinking *let me at 'em!* There are lots of stories of Yorkies "taking care of" a rat-infested barn or that mouse nest under the house. Don't be misled by their small size; many Yorkies are excellent hunters even today.

ENVIRONMENT

Yorkies make wonderful city dogs because they do very well in apartments, needing less exercise than many other breeds. They can be a city-dwelling

Train your children how to properly interact with their pet Yorkie.

fashionista's delight, tolerant and willing to be red carpet arm candy, but they also make great country dogs, tapping into their inner hunter. The portable Yorkie does well in just about any environment.

EXERCISE REQUIREMENTS

Yorkies are active small dogs. They thoroughly enjoy a daily walk but are small enough to also get their exercise from a vigorous ball game or game of tug-of-war in the backyard. Yorkies basically want to be with their owners. A mountain hike? Sure. Race up and down a long hallway, chasing a ball? Absolutely. This breed is great for the country or the city; he can adjust his exercise requirements to his owner's needs.

GROOMING REQUIREMENTS

Yorkies do have long hair and so require more grooming than a short-coated breed. Many people have their Yorkies trimmed with a puppy clip, where all the hair is cut regularly to 1 or 2 inches (2.5 or 5 cm). But Yorkie grooming can be surprisingly easy, even in full coat. Their hair is straight and strong, with very little undercoat. If you can spare 15 minutes a day to brush your dog, your Yorkie can have a shiny blue and tan coat flowing almost to the ground.

TRAINABILITY

For a breed made up of independent thinkers and original characters, the Yorkshire Terrier is remarkably trainable. They can also solve problems that their owners did not foresee (and sometimes even solve a problem that their owner never had). Yorkies need to be trained with a light touch and lots of variety because they can definitely get bored. They exhibit quick reaction times, have a good sense of humor, and above all enjoy taking care of their owner.

Dog Tale

Yorkie owner Sandy Fetchko relates a story about her problem-solving dog:

"Jake, one of our first Yorkies, was very smart and didn't like to share his toys. One day we were playing fetch and I was throwing the toy down the hall where he had to pass by the water dish. I watched him gaze wistfully at the dish as he went by. On his return trip he looked around to make sure none of the other dogs was watching and darted in behind the door to hide the toy. He ran to the dish, had a drink, and then ran back and got his toy to resume his return. Moral of the story—Yorkies problem solve! Problem: I'm thirsty but don't want the others to have the toy. Solution: Hide the toy so that I can have a drink. He was one smart little cookie."

The portable Yorkie does well in just about any environment.

Many have even achieved advanced obedience degrees. Their ability to jig and jag in pursuit of a mouse also allows them to do well and enjoy agility, a sport in which a dog is required to race through a series of obstacles.

Is the Yorkshire Terrier actually any harder to housetrain than a bigger dog? Anecdotally, all small dogs are harder to housetrain than their bigger cousins. But no one has done a real study on this. When a Lab puppy makes a mistake, everyone is galvanized to do something about it because the mess is larger. But when a Yorkie puppy potties in the house, many owners don't feel the same way because the mess is small. Then this becomes a habit, and that habit is indeed very hard to eliminate. The best thing is to follow housetraining rules exactly, right from the beginning. Then your Yorkie can be a clean dog for the rest of his life.

WATCHDOG ABILITY

Yorkies make good watchdogs. They are not as yappy as some other terriers but will enthusiastically bark when they feel that there is something to bark about. They are protective of their homes and courageous—most would not hesitate to let a burglar know in no uncertain terms that the thief is not welcome.

The Yorkshire Terrier is a big dog in a small package, tolerant of children and other dogs if well socialized, and more trainable than you would think. Loyal but quite independent, he is a bright and cheerful sprite clothed in a lovely mantle of blue and gold. No wonder he is so popular!

CHAPTER 3

SUPPLIES FOR YOUR
YORKSHIRE TERRIER

The Yorkshire Terrier has been known from the start as a "fancy" terrier. It may seem that this lovely morsel of blue and tan needs only the very best of the best—the best hair ribbons, the most satiny pillows, the highest-quality gourmet dog food have all seemed de rigueur for this elegant creature. From the London shops at the end of the 19th century specializing in pale blue leather Yorkie booties to the present day, Yorkie owners have consistently snapped up high-end goodies for their special dogs. Spoiling the ones we love can be a delightful pastime, and who better to shop for than our splendid companions?

But do Yorkies really need "the best of the best"? Not at all. Remember Smokey, the heroine of the Pacific Front in WWII? She camped out with her Bill during the war and slept in his helmet. She happily shared his K-rations. Yes, Yorkies need stuff, and you can definitely make your dog's life easier by having the correct equipment. But in buying this "one of a kind" bauble or that super-exclusive piece of equipment, remember whom you are buying it for—and, hint—it's not your dog. All that your Yorkshire really wants is your love and attention. Everything else is just gravy.

BED

Have you ever watched your Yorkie stalk a lizard? He sees his prey. Freezes. Crouches, waiting. Slowly moves toward it, waiting for exactly the right second—and pounces.

Yorkshire Terriers are "mousers" as opposed to "ratters." This behavior distinction explains a lot about the way they act. Ratters, such as Border Terriers and Jack Russell Terriers, attack their prey loudly and aggressively. Yorkies, on the other hand, are "watchers." They see the object of their desire and freeze,

Yorkies love a comfortable bed.

Your Yorkie's bed should be durable and washable.

waiting for exactly the right moment to attack. This means that they love having comfortable spots in the house from which to watch you.

Even though Yorkies are "fancy terriers," they are still dogs, subject to doggy pastimes. All dog beds need to be thoroughly washable, suitable for everything from a quick swipe to those times when your dog decides to roll in something interesting, then come in and take a nap.

Also remember that even the sweetest and best dog will sometimes get an urge to nibble. Dog beds don't last forever. When they get a hole in them, either sew the hole up promptly or throw the bed away. Dogs can get sick from eating stuffing or can get a limb caught in a loose string or a hole.

Dogs, even little guys like the Yorkshire, use their mouths similarly to how we use our hands. They fetch, carry, and arrange things with their jaws. (You would too if you had no thumbs.) Dogs are inherently rougher on their things than humans are. Therefore they should have things made for them, not hand-me-downs from us.

Any retail store selling dog supplies will also sell dog beds. Even the cheapest of stores will sell relatively sturdy and well-made ones.

DONUT BEDS

A favorite Yorkie bed is the simple but highly practical "donut." Shaped like an actual donut, the sides keep out the drafts, and there is a usually a removable cushion in the "hole." The inner cushion can be washed.

SATIN CUSHIONS

If you want to try to grow your Yorkie's coat as long as possible, satin cushions are helpful. They don't catch or break the coat as much as cotton or other fiber mixes can. Sometimes these cushions can be hard to find; if you are handy with a sewing machine, they are easy to make.

MINIMALIST BEDS

There are also beds that are made of a stretch of fabric over four legs composed of PVC pipes. Although this type of bed looks more like a bench than a bed, Yorkies in hot climates love them because the elevated design allows nicely for cooling air circulation.

UNCONVENTIONAL BEDS

Any regular throw pillow can and will be commandeered by your Yorkie as his bed. Sometimes Yorkies like to sleep on big stuffed animals as well. On the other end of the spectrum, if you want to go fancy, there are even dog beds that have

If your Yorkie prefers to sleep in your bed, make sure that he can climb up and down easily by himself.

headboards and ones that look like miniature sofas. These can cost as much as $250.00 or more.

YOUR BED

And what about sleeping on a real bed—that is, yours? Most Yorkies will jump at the chance to sleep on your bed if you allow it. If they are too small to make it all the way up, there are carpeted bed stairs you can

PUPPY POINTER

How do you get puppies used to new equipment? Slow and easy wins the race. Show your dog the scissors or comb, for example. If he is leery, let him get close to it, then move away and come in close again. Give your puppy time to check out whatever it is on his own schedule. If something completely freaks him out, leave it and come back to it later.

purchase to make the road a bit easier. But in that case, beware of having your dog jump off the bed, as it's probably too high and the chances for injury will be great. The rule of thumb is that if he can't climb onto it by himself, he won't be able to jump off it safely by himself.

COLLAR

A Yorkshire doesn't wear a collar all the time when he is in a full show coat. All collars break the coat somewhat, and nothing must get in the way of that flowing headpiece. But in day-to-day life with doors that get left open and gates that don't get latched, a Yorkie needs a collar.

HOW TO CHOOSE THE RIGHT SIZE

In dog supply catalogs and at pet stores, collars are sized by the inch. How do you tell which one is right? The only real way is to try it on your dog. You could need anywhere from an 8-inch (20-cm) to a 14-inch (36-cm) collar for a Yorkshire Terrier depending on his size, the collar manufacturer, and the type of collar.

The collar needs to be loose enough to slide easily on your dog's neck but not so loose that he could wiggle out in a panic. Pull the collar up tight under his chin and try to pull it over his head; if you can manage, the collar is too big.

TYPES OF COLLARS

There are a few different types of collars that are appropriate for the Yorkie.

Leather

The collar that breaks coat the least is rolled leather. This collar is cylindrical, with one seam rather than the usual two edges. These sturdy collars are a bit more expensive than the usual but well worth it.

Nylon

Nylon collars are soft and comfortable. If your Yorkie is in a Schnauzer or puppy clip, this is a good, inexpensive choice. However, if you are trying to keep your dog in full coat, a nylon collar will tend to break it.

High-End

High-end collars usually have some sort of gemstones or rhinestones attached and can be very expensive indeed. Because they break the coat more than any other collar, they would only be useful to match your three million dollar Winston diamond necklace when you are stepping out with your Yorkie to your latest film premiere. No film premieres in your future? Skip the gemstone collar.

Harnesses

What about harnesses? Yorkies can be stubborn imps, bound and determined to be in charge on walks, so harnesses are often recommended for them. But a harness tends to teach a dog to pull. Sled dogs know this—they can maximize their pulling abilities by pushing all their power against a central chest strap. Harnesses have their place with Yorkies who have neck or trachea problems, but a dog who hauls on the leash needs to learn his manners.

There are collars that attach onto a dog's muzzle, much like a horse's bridle, called no-pull harnesses. The theory is that if you can turn the dog's head, you can stop the pulling. They can be looked into for a dog who loves to pull.

CRATE

Dogs are hardwired to be den animals—they feel safe and comfortable in small, enclosed spaces. Even big dogs can and will squirm into the teensiest of nooks, turn around three times, sigh, and fall asleep. Yorkshires are the same, as any owner will tell you who has frantically scoured the house for her dog only to find him snoozing away at the bottom of a large pile of cushions.

Dog crates are not the torture devices they are sometimes made out to be. A

BE AWARE!
Where should your Yorkie be in the car? Yorkies, or any other dog for that matter, need to be in the backseat, either in a rigid crate or a dog harness car seat. They should never be in the front seat because an airbag deployment would kill them.

trained dog will often choose to sleep in his crate, even with the door open. A crate or dog carrier can be a godsend, allowing a well-mannered dog to travel anywhere his peripatetic owner might choose to go. And if your perfect Yorkie is not so thrilled around the grandchildren, a crate allows everyone to coexist comfortably.

HOW TO CHOOSE THE PROPER SIZE

A crate is the correct size when it allows your dog to stand up and turn around comfortably. A crate can definitely be too big—if it's big enough for your Yorkie to walk several steps, he may decide that it's convenient to sleep in one corner and go potty in the other. Once "trained" by you to do this, it's very hard to break the habit.

CRATE TYPES

There are a few different types of crates.

Wire

Found at most pet stores and online supply outlets, a wire crate lets air circulate easily and gives your dog visual access to his surroundings. However, they are not good for containment in a car because such a crate could be a death trap in an accident—the wire ends could break away from their welding and turn into sharp spears.

Wire crates allow air to circulate easily and give a dog visual access to his surroundings.

Plastic, Metal, or Wooden

These crates are rigid and excellent for all sorts of travel. They are very safe because they aren't easily crushed in an accident. There is even a story of an airplane crash in South America where the only survivor was a German Shepherd who was traveling in cargo—in a rigid plastic crate. Also, don't forget that dogs are den animals who like small enclosed spaces. Often dogs who are nervous and worried in a wire crate will calm down in a fully enclosed one. Such a crate feels more like a comforting den.

Plastic crates are rigid and excellent for all sorts of travel.

Soft-Sided Crates

These are made of nylon and PVC pipes. They break down easily and so are very convenient for travel. They are pretty lightweight, though, and some determined Yorkshires can turn them into a "turtle"—that is, they can move the crate across the room from the inside by whacking repeatedly on the walls.

Carry Bags

Yorkies are well known as take-along dogs. Their strong desire to go with their owners, as well as their small size, makes them an ideal everywhere buddy. But even the smallest of dogs sometimes needs containment; basically they need a bag of the correct size with sturdy handles. Many large women's purses are plenty big enough. Most high-fashion designers make purses that are big enough to carry a Yorkshire. They can also carry big price tags of several thousand dollars. But any big purse—even one without a logo—will do.

Airline Bags

Airline bags are somewhat different because the dog needs to be completely enclosed. An ideal airline bag has wheels and a telescoping handle. It's small on the top and expands to a flat bottom, with lots of mesh for good circulation. If upright, the dog can sit up. When the carrier is prone under the seat in front of you, he can stretch out.

Specialized Crates

Rigid crates made out of mahogany or custom made to match the rest of the furniture are definitely available. They can be lovely pieces of craftsmanship and carry pretty stunning price tags. An inexpensive alternative is crate covers; they are usually quilted, with a hole for the handle. They are pretty, do a good job of keeping out drafts, and are not expensive.

DOGGY GATE

Containment systems, even for portable dogs like the Yorkie, are a must. Sometimes there is a room in the house with expensive and breakable bric-a-brac. Other things, like the white leather sofa in the living room or the beautiful Oriental rug in the den, can be ruined by smelly tracked-in mud. Gates keep your Yorkshire safe and in an area where he will cause minimal damage in a worst-case scenario. This will help keep your blood pressure down and make puppy training and housetraining all that much easier. After all, would you prefer to tell your dog all the time what he is doing wrong or train him in a restricted area until he knows how to do things right?

Gates range from simple affairs put in with pressure clamps or hooks to stunning custom-made wrought iron or finely crafted wooden masterpieces. The simpler gates are great for temporary containment, to aid in housetraining, or to keep your dog in one room when you are away. The permanent ones can be a real asset not only to household peace but to the all-over decor. The permanent gates can also be surprisingly affordable.

Stainless steel bowls are sturdy and easily cleaned.

FOOD AND WATER BOWLS

Food and water bowls should be sturdy enough to manage an occasional whack and shove. Stainless steel bowls are a good choice because they are unbreakable and can be sterilized in the dishwasher, but those without weighted bottoms can be overturned. Ceramic food and water bowls are also a good choice, although they could shatter if dropped. But make very sure that the glazes don't contain lead, as this is every bit as toxic to dogs as it is to humans. Mexican-style ceramics often use lead-based glazes. Plastic bowls are not an ideal choice—they can harbor bacteria and aren't as sturdy as the other two types.

It's very nice to have a sturdy stainless steel water bowl in your dog's crate. That way if he needs to hang out there for several hours—say, while dog-allergic Aunt Mildred is visiting—he can drink when he chooses. The best kind of bowl sits in a ring that is clamped to the crate door and is removable.

GROOMING SUPPLIES

Even if you don't plan to do all of your Yorkshire's grooming yourself, you should have the following:

- 4" or 5" (10- or 13-cm) scissors. You can get scissors with blunt ends if you'd like; it will give you confidence that you're not about to stab your dog. By the way, you won't stab your dog, but it can take a while to gain this confidence.
- 4" or 5" (10- or 13-cm) thinning shears, teeth on one side only. These take out less coat than double-sided thinning shears.
- Good shampoo and conditioner. Because Yorkshires have hair as opposed to fur, good human hair products can work surprisingly well. The human products are often much less expensive than dog shampoos and conditioners. You'll also need a good leave-in conditioner. Leave-ins intended to detangle children's hair work well on a Yorkshire. There are also quite a few excellent canine leave-in conditioners from various companies.
- Greyhound-style metal comb. The good ones are fairly expensive because they will have few or no burrs to catch the coat. The purpose of such a comb is to check for tangles, not pull them out.
- Grooming arm. Yorkshire Terriers can be wriggly. A grooming arm

A grooming table may be helpful in holding your Yorkie steady while you groom him.

holds at least their head in place. You clamp the arm on the edge of a table. Grooming arms can be found on pet supply websites.

- A grooming table may be helpful. You don't really have to have this, but you need a comfortable place to groom your dog. You'll definitely require some sort of nonslip surface so that he feels secure on the surface. A nonslip bathmat works well for this.
- Hair bands and ribbons. To keep your Yorkie's hair out of his face, he will need either to have his eyebrow hair trimmed or wear a rubber band to hold his topknot up. You can get the small rubber bands needed at a good drugstore. Bows to go over the rubber band can be purchased online at most dog supply stores.
- Nail clippers. Get the kind for the biggest breeds. They are more powerful and therefore easier even on small toenails.
- Natural bristle brush, with or without plastic centers. If it has plastic centers, the plastic should not have a knob at one end, as the knob can break the coat. A natural bristle brush is good for brushing your dog's coat out once it is free of tangles.
- Small slicker brush. You want a small, fairly flexible one. If the tines are too stiff, they tend to be scratchy. These are good for brushing out feet hair.
- Stiff pin brush for tangle teasing. Basically it needs to be stiff enough to scratch an itch. Softer pin brushes are good as well, but they smooth the coat rather than detangle.

If your Yorkie is in a puppy or Schnauzer clip, he just needs shampoo and conditioner, leave-in conditioner, a nonslip surface on which to groom, nail clippers, a bristle brush with plastic centers, and a soft pin brush.

So you've gotten all your grooming equipment—and probably spent more than you intended. (Don't worry—it will all last a long time.)

IDENTIFICATION

Who owns your dog? Well, you do. But how can you prove this? And why would you want to? If your dog ever gets loose, you need to be able to prove that he is yours. Especially with a small dog with maximum cuteness factor—don't forget, he is a "fancy" terrier—you may someday run into somebody who thinks that she would like to own your dog. But with conclusive identification, you can prove who the real owner is.

MICROCHIPS

Microchipping is one form of identification. Microchips have a tiny chip embedded in a rice-grain-sized pellet of glass. (Glass is used because it won't irritate your Yorkie's system.) The chip is placed under a dog's skin with a syringe. It has a tiny hook on one side that locks it in place, so once injected between your Yorkie's shoulder blades, it will stay there.

Should your Yorkshire be microchipped? Absolutely. Anyone who has experienced the terror of losing a dog will tell you this. You should also have ID tags on your dog, but collars can be slipped out of or even removed. Your dog's chip is your ultimate proof that he is who you say he is.

A microchip provides irrefutable evidence that your dog is yours should he ever become lost or stolen.

TAGS

Some owners don't want to weigh down their little dogs and don't put any tags on their collars. Others attach so many that the dog sounds as if he's wearing castanets. A Yorkshire really needs a maximum of three tags:

- A rabies tag: If your dog is picked up by animal control, the officers will know that he has had his shots and so won't quarantine him if he has bitten anyone. They can also find you via his tag records.
- A microchip tag: Not only does such a tag mean that your dog is chipped, but a microchip tag signals to a casual person finding your lost dog that this is a loved and cared-for animal whose owner desperately wants him back.
- An ID tag: Chances are, if your dog gets loose he will be picked up by a neighbor or stranger long before he is seen by anyone with access to microchip or rabies records. If your name and telephone number are on a tag, a Good Samaritan can call you that much quicker.

Something to watch for in coming years is GPS tags. Even the most social dog, finding himself stranded in "the big outside," may panic and hide. This can make him extremely difficult to find. GPS tags allow you to track your dog. They do exist now but are too big for a small dog's collar and are quite expensive. Hopefully, in coming years they will become smaller and less expensive.

LEASH

Yorkies basically need two types of leashes.

WALKING LEASHES

These are usually pretty short, 4 to 6 feet (1 to 2 m), and very simple, either nylon or leather. Walking leads are for taking a dog for a walk at your side. Make sure that the clasp snap is small, as sometimes they can be pretty heavy. Don't use a retractable leash to walk your dog; it will give him too much range of motion and could result in injury for you or your dog if he suddenly tries to take off.

RETRACTABLE LEASHES

Heading to the park or a big field? A retractable leash allows your Yorkie to romp about with a degree of freedom. The handle of a retractable leash is plastic, and a nylon line is rolled inside with a spring, which is then attached to a regular leash. You can let your dog run more freely at the end of his leash (maximum lengths can be 8 or 10 feet [2.5 or 3 m]) and then reel him back in as needed. Here is where lots of range of motion is great!

ODOR-REMOVING CLEANSER

Even the cleanest of Yorkies can sometimes smell "doggy," and every once in a while even the best-trained dog will make a mistake. An essential part of any canine household is some sort of excellent odor-removing cleaning agent and an

Your dog should have a regular walking leash for taking a stroll with you.

air freshener spray. Especially if you have more than one dog, you may want to consider an air filter. The good ones work very well but tend to be fairly expensive.

TOYS

Yorkies love their toys. Like small children, they can never have enough of them. Toys come in several categories:

STUFFED

These toys should be made for dogs, not humans. Stuffed toys made for dogs tend to be much sturdier. If Mr. Bear happens to get a hole, make sure to sew him up quickly or throw him away—your Yorkie can get caught in the hole.

SQUEAKY

Dogs love things that squeak. Some Yorkshires will squeak squeak squeak squeak a toy until they can get at the squeaker and destroy it. But squeakers may have small parts that can lodge in your dog's intestines, requiring surgery. If you notice that your dog is digging for the squeaker, take the toy away. Instead of squeaky toys, try either stuffed animals without a squeaker or hard rubber ones.

Yorkies love their toys, and like children, can never have enough of them!

HARD RUBBER

These are the "unkillable" type of toy. Often your Yorkie won't be interested in this toy until it loses its "new" smell. Usually the toys have hollow middles, making them ideal goodie delivery devices. Stick in some kibble mixed with peanut butter and watch your Yorkie work on the toy until he has managed to get every slick of food out of it. Hard rubber toys filled with yummies are great for keeping your dog happy and occupied for hours.

X-PEN

An x-pen, or exercise pen, is a metal or nylon enclosure without a floor where your Yorkie can relax or even do his business. The less expensive x-pens can be adequate but are often heavier. Nylon ones can get considerably dirtier than their metal counterparts and need to be hosed down regularly. If you will be gone too long to be comfortable leaving your Yorkshire in his crate, you can put him in such a pen, with a bed in one corner and a potty station in another. Or you can carry an x-pen with you when you travel so that your dog will have a secure spot to go no matter where you are. Some x-pens have covers; if your Yorkie is a climber, this is an excellent idea.

Many Yorkies, even if they potty outside, are also trained to eliminate on papers. Yesterday's newspaper has been used for this ever since the little guys hung out under milady's skirt in Victorian England. Piddle pads have emerged in the last 15 years; they are certainly more absorbent than newspapers but can slide on a smooth surface if not somehow anchored. In the last five years, doggy litter boxes have come on the market; they work well but require more training to be effective.

The correct equipment can definitely make you and your Yorkie's life easier, and yes, it can be fun to buy the baubles as well!

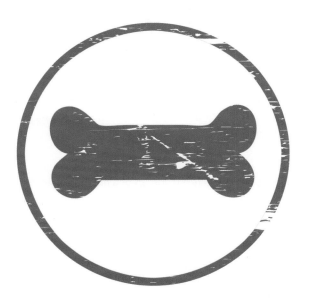

FEEDING YOUR
YORKSHIRE TERRIER

A Yorkshire Terrier needs a very specific mix of foods to do well. He requires certain nutrients to maintain his magnificent coat, enough energy to keep him going all day long, and a texture to his food that reduces tartar.

NUTRITION BASICS

Feeding your Yorkie right is much more than just supplying him with consumable energy. He needs the correct nutrition, which is the science of which foods are needed for optimum vigor, health, and longevity.

CARBOHYDRATES

Carbohydrates are organic compounds occurring in foods; they include sugars, starch, and cellulose and can usually be broken down to release energy. So carbs give your Yorkie the vitality he needs for all his important activities. Especially good are the complex carbohydrates in the form of rice, wheat, corn, or potatoes. Carbs should form about 50 percent of your Yorkie's diet.

FATS

Fat is a greasy organic substance made up of a mixture of lipids. Yorkies need fat, especially omega-3 and omega-6 fatty acids. Fats not only help provide the energy needed to keep him hopping but also prevent a dull, brittle coat and have an anti-inflammatory effect. Sufficient fat in a Yorkshire's diet (ideally between 16 percent and 18 percent of total nourishment) keeps his hair shafts smooth and strong, which aids in detangling. Omega-3s come from fish and flaxseed oils, and omega-6s come from seed and nut oils. The two fatty acids must be in correct balance.

Fats in the diet provide energy and help keep the coat shiny.

PROTEINS

Proteins are natural substances made up of amino acids. They are essential to the structure and function of all living cells and also supply long-lasting energy. Skin and hair renewal account for about 35 percent of protein requirements in an adult dog. A Yorkie needs quality protein and plenty of it to maintain his glorious coat and supple skin. His food should be between 25 and 30 percent protein.

VITAMINS AND MINERALS

Vitamins are organic substances essential, in small amounts, to regular body function. A Yorkie requires plenty of complex B vitamins to maintain his coat and condition. Biotin, known as the skin vitamin, is especially important. Sources of Vitamin B are animal-based products such as liver, turkey, and tuna, as well as potatoes, bananas, lentils, beans, brewer's yeast, and molasses. Other vitamins such as glucosamine for joint health and vitamin E work in conjunction with the B complex not only to help maintain current health but also to prevent degenerative conditions in the future.

Minerals are inorganic substances such as calcium or phosphorus that are necessary, in small amounts, for optimum metabolism. Yorkies need both calcium and phosphorus. To keep his long coat shiny and strong, he also needs trace minerals (iron, copper, zinc, and manganese) to jumpstart enzyme reactions.

WATER

There is one other necessary element here: water. All dogs need regular access to clean water. Just as with humans, water is essential to good health.

DOG FOOD LABELS

There are two main parts of a dog food label.

1. **The guaranteed analysis:** The guaranteed analysis is a certified breakdown of the constituent parts of the dog food. When comparing two different dog foods, the key percentage is the amount of moisture, as this affects the percentages in the rest of the analysis.

2. **The ingredients:** The ingredients must be listed from first to last according to the order in which they provide the greatest percentage of the weight of the product. Ideally, a protein should be the first ingredient. However, to make the formula look better, companies often divide up an ingredient considered less desirable into several subcategories, bringing them farther down the list.

A Yorkie needs more calories than most dogs his size; although small, he is busy and active.

Some often-misunderstood ingredients on a label include:

- **Meat by-products** are parts of the animal, not including meat proper. They include organs, blood, bone, and some fatty tissue. They do not include hair, horns, teeth, or hooves.
- **Poultry by-products** are clean parts of the chicken such as heads, feet, and organs. They do not contain feathers.
- **Brewer's rice** is fragmented rice kernels separated from milled rice. Brewer's rice, which contains the whole kernel, is healthier than the milled or "white" rice.
- **Beet pulp** is the dried residue of sugar beets added for fiber and palatability.
- **Corn gluten meal** is the dried residue left after the removal of bran, germ, and starch.
- **Animal digest** is a dried broth (think bouillon cubes) of any animal matter, excluding hooves and feathers.

YORKIE FEEDING CONSIDERATIONS

Some Yorkies enjoy nibbling dry dog food all day long. Others do better with a small amount of quality canned food put into dry food, with a bit of warm water added. Some like one completely dry meal and one with canned. Your Yorkie needs to enjoy his food enough to be willing to eat it. But there are many additional factors as well.

CALORIE REQUIREMENTS

A Yorkie needs more calories than most dogs his size. Although small, he is busy and active, and because of his low hair density, he is more susceptible to temperature changes than most other dogs. A good calorie benchmark for Yorkie nutrition is about 450 calories a cup. This is a chart of the amount of food an adult Yorkie needs a day, depending on how much he weighs:

Weight	Weight Maintenance
1 lb (.5 kg)	1/4 cup
3 lb (1.5 kg)	1/4 cup
5 lb (2.5 kg)	1/3 cup
8 lb (4 kg)	1/2 cup
10 lb (5 kg)	2/3 cup
12 lb (5.5 kg)	2/3 cup
15 lb (7 kg)	3/4 cup

Keep in mind that this is an average and can go up or down depending on your adult Yorkie's activity level.

PICKY EATING

Everyone knows that dogs can smell many times better than humans. Less well known is that their sense of taste is not as well developed—although perhaps a dog's choice in garbage appreciation is an indicator of this.

Dogs "taste" primarily through their sense of smell, but different breeds can smell things better or worse depending, in part, on the size of their noses. German Shepherd Dogs, for example, have 200 million olfactory cells in their noses, while Yorkies have only 60 million. Their lack of olfactory cells inhibits a

Yorkies have a tendency to be finicky eaters.

Yorkie's ability to taste. Smell is highly linked to taste, as anyone who has ever had a head cold discovers. It's no wonder, then, that your Yorkie can be a finicky eater. Therefore he needs dog food that is highly palatable.

YORKIE TEETH

A Yorkie's jaw is quite small, yet his teeth are relatively large, and he has a lot of teeth crowded into a relatively small area. He also has less bone in his jaw to support his teeth than larger breeds. The Yorkie comes from a terrier background, where big bad wolf-sized teeth were bred for hundreds of years so that the dog could grab that rabbit or rat as quickly as possible. Bred smaller first by pub owners looking for scrappy terriers as small as possible for their rat pits, then by breeders looking to maximize his small size and sterling locks, the Yorkshire has maintained relatively large teeth in a small jaw. His teeth can loosen and fall out with even a small amount of gum disease, so extra work must be taken to maintain them.

Your Yorkie needs a special diet to prevent tartar, gum disease, and tooth loss at an early age. He requires a small-sized kibble because the big chunks are too hard for him to chew. The kibble should have the correct amount of abrasion to loosen tartar.

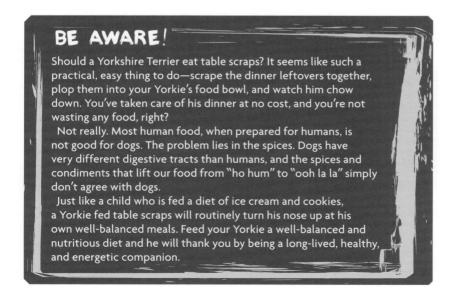

BE AWARE!

Should a Yorkshire Terrier eat table scraps? It seems like such a practical, easy thing to do—scrape the dinner leftovers together, plop them into your Yorkie's food bowl, and watch him chow down. You've taken care of his dinner at no cost, and you're not wasting any food, right?

Not really. Most human food, when prepared for humans, is not good for dogs. The problem lies in the spices. Dogs have very different digestive tracts than humans, and the spices and condiments that lift our food from "ho hum" to "ooh la la" simply don't agree with dogs.

Just like a child who is fed a diet of ice cream and cookies, a Yorkie fed table scraps will routinely turn his nose up at his own well-balanced meals. Feed your Yorkie a well-balanced and nutritious diet and he will thank you by being a long-lived, healthy, and energetic companion.

HYPOGLYCEMIA

Yorkies are susceptible to a condition called hypoglycemia, a sudden drop in glucose (sugar) in the dog's system. This can occur in stressed or very active dogs and especially in Yorkie puppies. Symptoms are a sudden loss of coordination, sleepiness, lack of appetite, and general weakness. Left untreated, it can lead to seizures, loss of consciousness, and death. For this reason, Yorkies must be fed more often than other dogs.

Because they are prone to hypoglycemia, a sudden drop in blood sugar, Yorkies must be fed more often than other dogs.

Yorkies are so small that they often have difficulty in storing sufficient glucose. Puppies are especially susceptible because they have very little by way of fat deposits, and the condition may also be connected to an immaturity in liver cells. Once he's weaned, feeding your up-to-2-pound (1-kg) puppy at least every four hours as well as 1/4 teaspoon of a high-calorie paste twice a day will help prevent this condition.

Because they can experience hypoglycemia, all adult Yorkies should be fed twice a day, and some do best on three times a day. They also require a special balance of highly palatable good-quality food. Complex carbohydrates such as whole grains are especially important because they break down into sugar slower than simple carbs. Carbohydrates from rice are best utilized; in descending order from rice in utilization potential are potato, corn and wheat, and oats and beans.

If you suspect that your Yorkie is having a hypoglycemic episode, don't panic. Immediately feed him a high-glycemic food such as corn syrup. If he can't eat, rub some syrup on his gums. Don't try to put food down his throat because he could choke. Keep him warm and call to inform your vet that you are bringing your dog in for immediate treatment; he may need intravenous glucose.

As soon as he starts to recover, give him a small meal high in protein, such as a beef- or chicken-based baby food, when you return home.

COMMERCIAL FOODS

Commercial foods are more than just convenient; they are a carefully crafted, well-researched balance of nutrition. All quality commercial dog foods are certified by the Association of American Feed Control Officials (AAFCO). Dog food companies spend millions of dollars researching the very best formulas for their foods. They do this for the simple reason that if they want their brand to sell well, it needs to work well. The best such foods can be an excellent resource for your Yorkie. But is commercial food the best option? That's for you to decide.

A Yorkie needs a particular nutritional mix of nutrients: protein levels between 26 percent and 30 percent, fat between 16 percent and 18 percent, carbohydrates about 50 percent, preferably complex ones for energy, and specific vitamins and minerals, like biotin, vitamin E, calcium, phosphorus, and copper. He also requires a small-sized kibble with the right amount of abrasion to control tartar.

There are commercial foods for puppies, seniors, and every sort of special situation and condition in between. There are also many mixes for allergies, kidney conditions, etc., that are sold only at your vet's office that are an excellent way to alleviate conditions or symptoms with nutrition rather than medication. Obviously, if your Yorkie has a medical condition, you should follow your vet's recommendations. Just remember that whatever you feed your dog, he has to like it; if he turns his nose up at a fancy vet dog food, he won't get the benefit from it.

DRY FOOD

Quality commercial dry dog foods, or kibble, are easy to use and out of the box ready to go, with a tartar-reducing texture. They also tend to be less expensive than noncommercial foods. To determine which dry food is right for your dog, ask yourself these questions:

1. Is this food right for Yorkies in general? Does it have the correct proportion and mix for the breed, which is meat as the first ingredient to provide around 30 percent protein, fat at between 16 percent and 18 percent, and carbohydrates at around 50 percent?
2. Which food does he prefer and eat well?
3. Which formula fits my pocketbook? Super-premium formulas tend to be about double the price of premium ones.
4. How active is my Yorkie? The higher protein and fat levels in some formulas might be too high if your dog is more couch potato than bounce-a-holic.

Buy small amounts of various brands until you and your Yorkie have hit upon the right mix. Actually, it's a good idea to always buy small bags rather than large ones because quality formulas often have limited preservatives and so can go bad quickly.

Dry food is easy to feed and has a tartar-reducing texture, a benefit for toy dogs, who are more prone to dental problems.

Dog Tale

Robbie almost had me buffaloed on the subject of treats. It all started with those fake bacon strips. Robbie loved them. Whenever I went into the kitchen, I'd give him one or two. It was a bit like buddies bonding over ice cream. But just like with ice cream, pretty soon Robbie didn't want to eat his regular food and started getting a bit round in the middle.

By then I was on a diet myself and trying to work a lot of healthy vegetables into the family regime. I discovered that every time I dropped a peeling on the kitchen floor, Robbie would vacuum it up and watch expectantly for more. Hmm! So I cut out the fake bacon pieces and replaced them with lots of fresh veggies. Robbie's favorite was broccoli. He and I would bond just as well with vegetables as treats; he had plenty of appetite left for the good stuff and soon was back in fighting trim form.

CANNED FOOD

Canned food looks as if it's only meat, but that's not true. It is a moist product and basically the same formula as dry dog food but with lots of liquid. Canned food can be useful as an addition to dry dog food because it mixes in well and can increase palatability. Yorkies love the taste, but if fed alone it won't reduce tartar buildup. Canned food is ideally used as a sort of gravy. Put a spoonful on top of kibble, add a small amount of warm water—which also increases palatability—and stir.

SEMI-MOIST FOOD

Semi-moist dog food is not as wet as canned. It is a highly preserved product about the consistency of soft fruit leather, re-formed generally into shapes like mock hamburger. Unlike canned, it cannot be used with dry food because it's not moist enough to be mixable. Used alone, it is too soft to help with tartar reduction and has a lot of sugar. Semi-moist dog food is not recommended for Yorkies.

NONCOMMERCIAL FOODS

Noncommercial foods are diets that you put together yourself for your Yorkie. They are usually set up according to some sort of formula but are generally not as precise as a commercial diet made up under rigorous guidelines in a factory.

HOME-COOKED DIET

Just as there is nothing better than a home-cooked meal, making your Yorkie's food yourself can be an option. Many owners prefer the higher-quality, human-grade ingredients they can serve their dog themselves rather than the possibly questionable ingredients and preservatives coming out of a dog food bag.

There are good recipes for homemade dog food available online. However, take care that the food served is consistently the correct nutritional mix for your Yorkie. Just as the right nutritional formula can extend your dog's life and keep him healthy and happy, the wrong one can significantly shorten his life span. When you make your dog's food yourself, the responsibility for his nutrition is entirely in your hands. Before choosing this type of diet, check with your veterinarian to make sure that a home-cooked diet is the right choice for your Yorkie.

RAW DIET

Proponents of a raw food diet claim that feeding dogs a natural mix of uncooked meat, ground raw bones, vegetables, and fruits is the most natural and therefore the best food for them (although controlled studies have not substantiated this claim). Proponents claim that a raw diet leads to stronger, healthier hair and skin and increased energy. However, there is concern about possible food poisoning attendant to eating uncooked meat, and your Yorkie's small digestive tract can become impacted by eating ground bones. Raw food can also spoil, opening up the possibility of salmonellosis or even botulism poisoning.

Raw diet proponents claim that such food is natural and therefore the best for dogs to eat.

Veterinary associations such as the American Veterinary Medical Association (AVMA), British Veterinary Association (BVA), and Canadian Veterinary Medical Association (CVMA) have warned of the animal and public health risk that could arise from feeding raw meat to pets and have stated that there is no scientific evidence to support the claimed benefits of raw feeding. If you're still considering a raw diet, check with your vet before beginning your Yorkie on this regimen.

TREATS

Commercial dog treats tend to be overprocessed, overly sweetened, and overpriced. Either your Yorkie won't really like them, making them a waste of money, or he'll like them too well and they'll spoil his appetite.

A great treat is a bone, but which kind to get? The best

idea is to purchase bones from a pet store; that way you know that they are appropriate to dogs and have been processed correctly. Some can be chewed on for months, and there is even a type that can be filled with kibble mixed with peanut butter for a gooey, long-lasting goodie. But the very best treats, and ones that don't spoil your Yorkshire's appetite, are veggies. Most dogs love fresh vegetables, especially broccoli, carrots, and the crunchy parts of lettuce. Be sure to cut them up small enough for your dog to chew on.

FREE FEEDING VERSUS SCHEDULED FEEDING

Yorkies are active little athletes who generally do not eat everything in the bowl all at once. Because of this, they do best with a mix of free feeding (leaving food out all day) and scheduled meals. Leave a bowl of dry food around where your dog can reach it during the day. He will nibble on this as he feels like it. Then serve him one to two scheduled meals a day containing dry food, with maybe a bit of canned food on top for increased palatability. (Canned dog food is apparently tastier at room temperature rather than frosty from the fridge.) Pick up the served meal after about half an hour.

OBESITY

Yorkies are not as prone to becoming overweight as many other small breeds are, but it can certainly happen. If your dog is starting to resemble a small football, he is probably overweight. But you need to do more than just feed him less. The problem with overweight dogs is that they are in the habit of eating a certain volume of food. If you don't feed them that amount, they will let you know.

Special dog foods that have fewer calories but the same amount of bulk are available for overweight dogs. You can also take the food that your Yorkie already loves too well and put in your own bulky but low-caloric additives. Popular are cooked green beans and plain air-popped popcorn. Veggies or long-lasting bones should be substituted for rich treats as well.

Your overweight Yorkie also needs to get more exercise. If he never goes on walks, now is the time to start. He can also chase a ball for 20 minutes in the backyard. It doesn't matter what you do—it's the movement that counts. Pretty soon the fat will come off and your Yorkie's energy level will increase.

A Yorkshire Terrier is a sturdy and energetic mighty mite, needing a very specific mix of nutrition, energy resources, and food textures to do his best. When fed correctly, your Yorkie will thank you with many years of healthy and happy companionship.

GROOMING YOUR
YORKSHIRE TERRIER

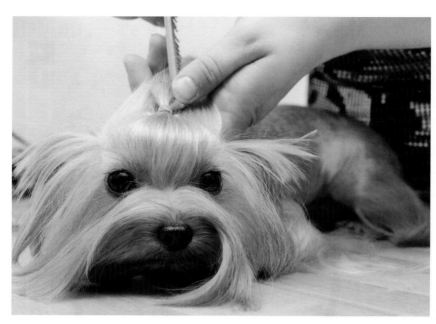

Grooming should be a relaxing time of interaction between you and your Yorkie.

There is nothing more beautiful than a satiny, shiny Yorkshire Terrier, his long hair flowing past his feet. Grooming is vital to create and take care of this glory. It can also be surprisingly easy if you know how to do it.

The beautiful image of a Yorkshire Terrier in full show coat is truly stunning. What a shame it would be if this image had to be abandoned entirely in the pet Yorkie! The fact is that if you can spend 15 minutes a day, every day, on your Yorkie's coat, you can keep him in his flowingly full long-coated condition. If that is too much you can always give him a Schnauzer cut or puppy clip. (See sidebars.)

WHY GROOMING IS IMPORTANT

Regular grooming in any breed, shorthaired or longhaired, is an important activity. A matted, dirty dog is more susceptible to infections than a clean and detangled one. Also, the time you spend grooming your dog allows you to check him for fleas or ticks. These pests can be addressed easily and eliminated—if caught quickly. Even serious medical conditions like tumors are best detected during grooming.

Grooming should be a relaxing time of interaction between you and your Yorkie. Most of us enjoy going to the hair salon and being pampered. Trained well and kindly, your dog will enjoy it as well.

Many owners think that only regular trips to the groomer will keep their dog in pristine condition. In Yorkies, the contrary is true. A Yorkshire needs about 15 minutes of daily grooming to maintain a full-length coat. Daily grooming means that owners need to learn how to do this themselves, but it's not difficult with the right techniques.

Grooming for the Schnauzer cut is a 15-minute brushing twice a week. For a puppy cut, where all the hair is cut to 1 inch (2.5 cm), it's a bath once a week.

GROOMING SUPPLIES

Grooming supplies for your Yorkshire need not be expensive. There are some surprising areas where corners can definitely be cut without sacrificing quality coat care. In other areas, the top-quality product really is the best one for the job.

4" OR 5" (10- OR 13-CM) SCISSORS

These can be purchased at a beauty supply store. You can get scissors with blunt ends if you'd like; they will give you the secure feeling that you're not about to stab your dog. By the way, you won't stab your dog, but it can take a while to gain this confidence.

4" OR 5" (10- OR 13-CM) THINNING SHEARS

Thinning shears can be helpful to trim stray hairs on the ears or around the feet. The more teeth the scissors have, the less hair they take out with each cut, so in this case more teeth is better.

The same blow-dryer you use on your own hair will work well on your Yorkie.

BLOW-DRYER

The same dryer you use on your own hair will work well on your Yorkie. You can make the dryer hands-free either by filling a jar with pebbles and sticking the dryer handle in it or by buying a blow-dryer arm that clamps to the side of the table from an online pet supply store.

BRUSHES

The general rule about brushes is this: the more coat you have to deal with, the larger the brush should be. But personal preference plays a role.

Big brushes are less handy and more expensive, but they are great if you have a Yorkshire in full coat, as one swoop takes you all the way down the side of the dog.

Here is a rundown of the brushes you'll need:

Boar and Nylon Brush

These can be used for light tangles and have more grip than a full boar bristle brush. (See below.) You can find good boar and nylon brushes at beauty supply stores. Just make sure that you get the kind that does not have a plastic knob at the end of the nylon bristle, as that tends to break the coat.

Full Boar Bristle Brush

This brush is basically to smooth down a coat that is already fully brushed. It is very good at gentle hair stimulation. You can get good full boar bristle brushes from beauty supply stores.

Nylon Brush

This brush should only be used when detangling. A sturdy and inexpensive

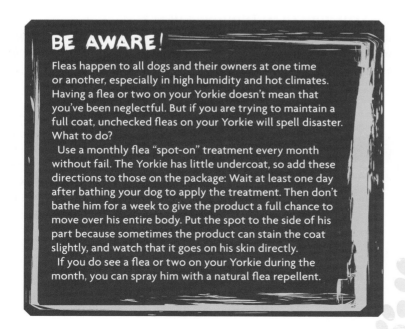

BE AWARE!

Fleas happen to all dogs and their owners at one time or another, especially in high humidity and hot climates. Having a flea or two on your Yorkie doesn't mean that you've been neglectful. But if you are trying to maintain a full coat, unchecked fleas on your Yorkie will spell disaster. What to do?

Use a monthly flea "spot-on" treatment every month without fail. The Yorkie has little undercoat, so add these directions to those on the package: Wait at least one day after bathing your dog to apply the treatment. Then don't bathe him for a week to give the product a full chance to move over his entire body. Put the spot to the side of his part because sometimes the product can stain the coat slightly, and watch that it goes on his skin directly.

If you do see a flea or two on your Yorkie during the month, you can spray him with a natural flea repellent.

brush will do fine. Nylon brushes can be purchased from a beauty supply store or a pet supply store.

Small Slicker Brush
These are good for brushing out feet and leg hair. The best soft slickers for a Yorkshire can be purchased from a good pet supply website.

Soft Pin Brush
Soft pin brushes work well to smooth the coat and to get out light tangles. These brushes go deeper than a boar and nylon brush but still have a smoothing function. They can be bought from most online pet supply websites.

Stiff Pin Brush
Stiff pin brushes with harder pads and shorter, stiffer pins will also detangle and are faster than using a nylon brush, although they will pull out more hair. They can be bought from most online pet supply websites

COMBS
You'll need two varieties of comb:

Greyhound-Style Metal Comb
The better-quality metal combs are more cost effective in the end. Cheap combs aren't totally smooth but have burrs on their teeth that can break the coat. This

Pictured is a selection of Yorkie grooming equipment. From the left, a soft pin brush, a full boar brush, a boar and nylon brush, a rat-tail comb, and two sizes of metal combs.

is one area where you need to buy the best. Greyhound-style combs can be purchased from online pet supply stores. The smaller metal combs are great as face and topknot combs.

Rat-Tail Comb

These need not be expensive and can be purchased from a beauty supply store. They are used to tease out tangles. Rat-tail combs are generally plastic and have a pick at the end that can help work out tangles.

CORDLESS TRIMMER

This is a small cordless clipper that can be purchased from an online pet supply store. Don't buy it from a beauty supply store because trimmers and clippers intended for humans have a high-pitched whine inaudible to us that dogs can hear—and in this case, they don't like what they hear. The trimmer is very helpful in taking the hair off the inside and back of your Yorkie's ears and sand out from between the pads of his feet. If you plan to do a Schnauzer or puppy clip, you'll need a regular pair of clippers as well.

How to Do a Schnauzer Clip

Fifteen minutes a day grooming a full-coated Yorkshire doesn't sound like a lot. But if life gets in the way and a couple of days get missed, your smooth and shiny dog can easily turn into one great big mat.

To give your Yorkie a Schnauzer clip, you'll need regular clippers and a 1-inch (2.5-cm) comb attachment. Run the clippers down the top of his back, then about halfway on the side of his body. This will clear off the majority of the really long coat while still giving the impression of plenty of length. The hair on the face is left pretty much as is because it generally doesn't get long enough to be bothersome.

DENTAL RUBBER BANDS

These are tiny rubber bands that are perfect for putting in topknots or to keep vent hair tied up and out of the way. They can be purchased at some drugstores or online from small-dog grooming supply stores.

GROOMING ARM

Small dogs can be wriggly. A grooming arm, clamped to the side of a table, holds at least the dog's head in place. You can get one at a pet supply website.

GROOMING TABLE

Do you really need a grooming table? No, but you need a comfortable, stable table, and you definitely need some sort of nonslip surface so that your dog feels secure. A nonslip bathmat works well for this.

NAIL CLIPPERS

Get the nail clippers made for the biggest breeds—they are more powerful and therefore easier even on small toenails. Scissor types are the best because it's easier to see the nail while you're trimming. There are also nail grinders on the market; they basically use a small revolving drum of sandpaper to grind down the nail. Dogs tolerate these much better than the nail clippers. But while they can be extremely useful with a short-coated dog, a wiggly Yorkie could easily get his long hair twisted into the revolving shaft of the nail grinder's drum, causing the hair to be pulled out by the roots. Use nail grinders with care.

SHAMPOO AND CONDITIONER

You can spend a great deal of money on top-notch dog shampoos that are of excellent quality and do a great job. And yes, the pH of dog hair is different from that of human hair. So in theory, human shampoos and conditioners shouldn't work well on dogs. Except they do. Human shampoos and conditioners work very well indeed with a Yorkshire Terrier, whose hair is after all very similar to human locks.

The best time to brush your Yorkie is after a bath, when he's damp, or after spraying him with a leave-in conditioner.

Because a Yorkie's coat always needs to be brushed damp, a spray bottle filled with some sort of leave-in conditioner is a must. Canine-only leave-ins can be purchased from online pet supply companies. Children's detangler spray conditioners also work well.

TOPKNOT BOWS

Ribbons hand-tied around the topknot rubber band last about five minutes before a normal Yorkie shakes them off. Sturdy topknot bows come ready-made, slip right over the rubber band, and stay there.

Sturdy ready-made topknot bows stay in place.

COAT AND SKIN CARE

Grooming is not just about making your Yorkie look good. A dirty, tangled dog can get skin rashes and infections. And problems like fleas can make him—and you—miserable. These things are among the reasons why it's so important to inspect the coat and skin regularly.

If any of the procedures in this section upsets your dog, don't immediately move to another. Give him a break. Then go on and perform the next action. Groomers don't have this luxury but you do.

BRUSHING

There are two old sayings in grooming:
1. Never brush a dog who's dry.
2. Never brush a dog who's wet.

Although they seem contrary, there is actually truth in both statements. It's true that one should never brush a dry dog. Tangles can be formed around dirt that will literally wash away once he is bathed. (Scratched or rubbed tangles combined with dirt won't wash out, but they still benefit from being cleaned and conditioned before being brushed out.)

If you brush a wet dog, you'll pull at the hair follicle when it's vulnerable, stretching and weakening it. So don't brush a dog who's wet. Ideally, you should brush your Yorkie when he's damp, either from a bath or by being lightly sprayed with a leave-in conditioner. However, it's better to brush a dog after being bathed if he is dirty.

How often should you brush a Yorkie? The answer, if you want to maintain a full coat, is every day—seven days a week, without fail. This will take about 15 minutes. If you have your Yorkie in a Schnauzer trim (see sidebar "How to Do a Schnauzer Clip"), he will need to be brushed a couple times a week; if he's in a puppy clip, it's once a week. (See sidebar "How to Do a Puppy Clip.")

How to Brush

Start with your dog belly up, either on the table or in your lap. Yes, he will need to get used to this position, and a typical Yorkie may not like it. Put a towel bunched under him to give him a bit more security.

Brush him out from the bottom up, belly and legs first, using the boar and nylon brush. Once your Yorkie gets the idea, he will like this and find it relaxing. You start out underneath the dog because otherwise it's far too easy to miss the small tangles, ending up with a dog who is smooth on top and tangled underneath—not a good thing.

Method One: Tangles happen. They happen to dogs with gorgeous long coats and short scruffy coats and everything in between. The idea is to catch tangles early, when they aren't a big deal. The loosest part of a tangle is at its bottom, so you want to loosen it from the bottom up. When you dig your brush into the top of a tangle and power downward, you are actually tightening the tangle and will pull out more hair that way. That is why it's more effective to work your way upward. You can either use a strong nylon brush for this or a stiff pin brush. The nylon brush will take longer but will take out less hair.

Method Two: First separate the tangle as much as you can by hand. Then take the pointed end of a rat-tail comb and pick out the rest. Take your time. Then brush the area out to make sure that you have gotten it all.

A note here about combs: Metal combs are good for checking for

Metal combs are good for checking for tangles.

tangles, but they are lousy for getting rid of them. They pull extra hair out and will leave your Yorkshire plotting revenge. Loosen tangles only with a stiff pin brush, nylon brush, or plastic rat-tail comb.

BATHING

How often should you bathe your Yorkie? Basically when he needs it, but as a general rule, bathe him once a week.

A note about ears: It is not a good idea to fill the ear canal with water. Fungus can easily grow in such a dark, wet environment. So before you start the bath, squirt a small amount of ear cleaner into each ear and follow up with a small amount of cotton wool. This will go a long way toward keeping the ears healthy and fungi-free. When the bath is over and you remove the cotton wool, clean the exterior portions of the ear that you can see with a cotton ball. (Never put anything into the ear canal.)

How to Bathe

It's easiest to bathe a Yorkshire in the sink—a hose attachment is quite helpful for this. If you don't have one, make do with a plastic cup until you replace your sink fixtures. Then get a faucet with a hose attachment.

Wet the dog down to the skin, then put the shampoo first in your hand and then on your dog; you'll have better control that way. Move the shampoo straight down the hair. You can easily tangle your dog's coat by scrubbing shampoo in a circular motion. Then rinse out the shampoo thoroughly; residue left after bathing can dull your Yorkie's coat.

Always use a conditioner after the shampoo has been completely rinsed out of the coat, and don't be stingy,

The general rule is to bathe your Yorkie once a week.

You'll need two towels to dry your Yorkie: one to carefully dry him to prevent tangling and one in which to wrap him afterward to soak up excess water.

especially if your dog's hair is tangled. Leave it in for a minute or two. It's helpful to have the conditioner sit in his hair for five minutes once a month. How do you keep him in the sink that long? Entertain him! Also, don't leave his side so that he knows he can't get away with jumping. Rinse the conditioner briefly, but be sure to leave the hair a bit slick.

You'll need two towels to dry your Yorkie. Use one to get the immediate water off him. Dry him by moving the towel over his hair in a downward direction, just as you did with the shampoo. Then wrap him in a fresh towel and put him into his crate to dry further for roughly 20 minutes.

Now what? Well, you can hear your Yorkie shaking vigorously, turning around in his crate, shaking again, and rubbing his beard dry against the towel. When he is no longer dripping, you can decide—to blow-dry or not to blow-dry?

BLOW-DRYING

If your Yorkie is in full coat, he should be blown out after every bath. Otherwise you just need to blow him out when you want him to look extra pretty. Once he is no longer dripping and is standing on a nonslip sturdy surface, you can start to blow him dry.

To start, spray on some kind of leave-in conditioner. This will help protect the coat from the heat of the dryer. You can use either a canine leave-in conditioner or a human one (usually marketed as children's detangler).

Blow-dry on a cool setting and brush, using a boar and nylon brush or a pin brush, from the bottom up, just as when you were brushing your Yorkie. Once his belly and legs are dry and tangle-free, continue blow-drying him from the top down. Make sure to really get under the topcoat to dry everything, and watch out for areas like behind the ears and on the cheeks and neck.

PUPPY POINTER

Yorkie puppies are born black with tan points. As they get older, their adult color grows out underneath, producing an adolescent coat of steel blue and tan, with black tips.

Puppies need coat care just like adult Yorkies to keep them tangle-free but also so that they learn that grooming can be a relaxing and pleasant activity. Grooming needs to be especially vigilant when the puppy is a "teen" between about 8 and 12 months old, as often there are lots more tangles as his full coat emerges.

Once he's dry, use a metal comb to part the coat, from the back of your Yorkie's head to the tip of his tail.

HAIR TRIMMING

The goal of trimming a Yorkshire Terrier, even one who is never going to see the inside of a show ring, is to make him look as if his hair just happened to grow that way.

The sound and feel of the trimmer can be frightening for your dog. Clippers make a strange noise, and they tickle. To get him accustomed to the clippers, place the tool on your dog's back, business end away from him. Let him feel the vibration as well as hear the noise. Give him treats as you do this to help him associate the clippers with something he loves.

Once your Yorkie is accustomed to the clippers, take your time when trimming his hair and do a little bit at a time so as not to frighten him.

Feet

Starting with his feet, trim the hair between his toes and the small bit behind his foot with the cordless clipper. On his front feet there is a knob; trim up to that. On the back feet trim just an inch or two (2.5 or 5 cm) up the back of his leg.

Once done with trimming his feet, run your scissors around the edge of his foot to make a neat package.

This is a correctly groomed foot.

Ears

Take the trimmers and run them first with the grain of the hair and then against the grain of the hair on the back of both ears about one-third of the way down. Then clipper the inside of the ears.

When you've clippered the ears, you can trim the edges. Just run your scissors around the ear edge where you have trimmed.

Tail Hair

Vent or tail hair can get dirty very quickly, but there is a simple technique to keep it out of the way: It can either be braided, or it can have multiple rubber bands tied around it. Trim carefully with scissors right around the anus to keep this sensitive area clear.

Topknot

Of all the Yorkshire Terrier's grooming, the topknot can seem the most daunting. Yes, it is certainly simpler to trim some of the hair around your Yorkie's eyes and a bit of his eyebrows to keep his eyes clear. But if you've gone to the trouble to keep your dog in a full coat, it's pretty easy to maintain the topknot once you know how.

First, take a small towel about the size of a dish towel. Roll it up on its short end and rubber band it so that it stays tight. Put it under your Yorkie's chin. It will help stabilize his head and relax him. Then to create the topknot:

To create the topknot (from left to right): 1.) First part the hair from the corner of the eye to the base of the ear on each side; 2.) then put on the first rubber band; 3.) pull up on some of the hair above the rubber band to tighten it; 4.) add a second rubber band; 5.) the bow then slides on between the two rubber bands.

1. First part the hair from the corner of the eye to the base of the ear on each side using the metal comb. Gently pull the hair you have collected up together.
2. Put on the first rubber band as if you are putting the hair in a ponytail.
3. Then pull up on some of the hair above the rubber band to tighten it.
4. Next add a second rubber band about 1 inch (2.5 cm) above the first one.
5. Finally, slide your bow on between the two rubber bands.
6. Voilà!

EAR CARE

Yorkies have a prick (pointed and erect) ear, which naturally stays much cleaner than a drop ear. Still, if not cared for properly, your dog's ears can get infected. If neglected and left untreated, he could even become deaf.

HOW TO CARE FOR THE EARS

Fungus can easily grow in ear canals, especially when they are also wet. This is why you should squirt a small amount of witch hazel into each ear and follow up with a small amount of cotton wool before you start a bath, which will help keep your dog's ears healthy and fungi-free. It will also prevent ear mites. When you have finished bathing your Yorkie, remove the cotton wool and use a cotton ball to clean the exterior portions of the ear that you can see. (Never put anything into the ear canal.)

EYE CARE

A Yorkie's eyes tear easily and are susceptible to infection. He has rounded, slightly almond-shaped eyes that are fairly prominent in his small face.

HOW TO CARE FOR THE EYES

Eye care is very simple but needs to be consistent. There's just one step: Clean the eyes daily with a sterile eye drop solution. Put a drop in each eye and gently wipe away any excess.

Dog Tale

I'm not sure that my dog Robbie ever enjoyed his bath, but he was very patient about it. He would generously accept my working him over meticulously in the big kitchen sink through the wetting down, shampoo, conditioner, and final rinse. If I got soap in his eyes he would shake his head vigorously, and he definitely didn't like water up his nose—but then, who does? He would snort and snort, then look up at me resentfully. But other than this, Robbie knew that this was a necessary procedure he needed to tolerate.

After I dried him thoroughly, I'd put him down and his pent-up energy would burst out. He'd race away at a dead gallop; I'd hear his pita-PAT pita-PAT, pita-PAT get softer and almost disappear as he headed toward the house's nether regions. There would be a few seconds of silence and then the pita-PAT would get louder and louder as he returned – and he would roar by. Think of the Doppler effect of a train passing—that was Robbie, now headed in the opposite direction. He would pass me like this five or six times before he would plop down at my feet with his tongue all the way out and a silly grin on his face. Oh, and this too—by then his hair was always dry.

If your dog hates getting his nails trimmed, try doing one foot at a time or even one nail at a time.

NAIL CARE

If your dog hates getting his nails trimmed, try doing one foot at a time or even one nail at a time, if that's what it takes. Try trimming a nail and then giving your dog a small treat so that he associates the experience with something positive. Then take a quick break and begin again.

If your dog decides that he absolutely will not get his nails trimmed under any circumstances, use a small nylon muzzle. A good muzzle doesn't restrict your dog in any other way than to keep his mouth closed. The muzzle simply lets him know that certain actions are currently physically impossible. You don't want to waste time dodging your Yorkie's teeth, and you don't want to inadvertently teach him that going after you is acceptable behavior.

Trim your Yorkie at the latest when he sounds like a tap dancer. This means that his toenails are hitting the floor, which affects his feet and therefore his posture. If you cut his nails every week after his bath, they will never become too long and he will consider the procedure routine and acceptable.

HOW TO TRIM THE NAILS

A toenail has a curve in it. This is where the "quick," a blood vessel running down your dog's nail, ends. Using the big-sized scissor-type nail clippers, cut the nail at the curve or a bit above and always at an angle toward the dog. Avoid the quick because if you nip it, you will make your dog's toenail bleed. But understand that if this occurs you don't need to head for the emergency room. Just apply some styptic powder or cornstarch to the nail to stop the bleeding.

DENTAL CARE

There are some breeds that naturally have healthy teeth, but Yorkies aren't one of them. Yorkies have relatively large teeth in a small jaw. They also have a lot of teeth crowded into a small jaw. If not cared for properly, the Yorkie can lose his teeth at a young age. Also, there is a definite medical connection between gum health and heart health; unchecked periodontal disease has been linked to cardiopathy. So tooth health is not just about maintaining his pearly whites—it's about the life of your dog.

An engaged owner willing to provide regular dental care can make a real difference. What kind of daily care? You must learn how to brush your dog's teeth. There are various products on the market that will get the job done: dog toothbrushes and even specialized brushes that fit on the end of your finger. Keep in mind that the toothpaste you choose must always be intended for dogs— human toothpaste is neither good for nor helpful to your Yorkie. For one thing, human toothpaste foams way too much, and it shouldn't be swallowed.

Your dog will probably also need regular teeth cleaning at the vet. Consult your vet as to how often this should occur.

How to Brush the Teeth

The wiggle factor in this procedure is seriously reduced by teaching your Yorkie to sit and lie down on command. (See Chapter 7.) Ideally, you should brush the teeth daily.

Start at the top and in the back of the mouth. Put a small amount of toothpaste on the toothbrush and brush the teeth as you would your own, using a circular motion and making sure to brush to the gum line. (Dogs don't need to have their teeth brushed on the inside, so that's not necessary.) Then brush the bottom teeth in the same fashion. If your Yorkie gets very squirmy with this, do the top teeth in one session and the bottom teeth in another.

New Developments in Dental Care

There are a couple of new developments in canine dental care:

Laser teeth cleaning. This is far more precise and less invasive than traditional veterinary dental care. Some vets are even performing the procedure without anesthesia, thus saving the extra expense, but even more importantly, the extra risk to the dog.

Dental products. Once your Yorkie's teeth are clean, there are several products on the market, put in either a dog's water or food, that will help keep his teeth clean. Some may be more effective than others.

Chew products. There are quite a few sticks or bones on the market designed to help reduce tartar. Use these in moderation because your dog will also be eating them, so they will contribute to—or detract from—his diet.

FINDING A PROFESSIONAL GROOMER

If you are planning to keep any kind of coat on your Yorkie, you have to learn some grooming techniques. Even in a modified Schnauzer trim, a Yorkie requires a thorough brushing every couple of days and a bath once a week, and in a puppy clip, still requires brushing and a bath once a week. But many people want their Yorkie to be trimmed professionally, regardless of cut.

HOW TO FIND A GROOMER

How do you find someone who will do a good job on your dog? There are several resources that can help.

- Ask your dog's breeder, if the breeder is local. Sometimes a breeder does grooming as well. If so, lucky you!
- Speak to any friends and neighbors who have long-coated dogs. Whom do they use?
- Often vets also have associated groomers. If you like your vet, you may like the vet's groomer.
- Check out the Yellow Pages, as well as online resources.

Your dogs vet may be able to recommend a good groomer.

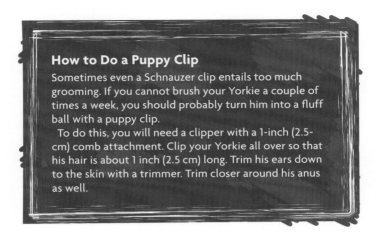

How to Do a Puppy Clip

Sometimes even a Schnauzer clip entails too much grooming. If you cannot brush your Yorkie a couple of times a week, you should probably turn him into a fluff ball with a puppy clip.

To do this, you will need a clipper with a 1-inch (2.5-cm) comb attachment. Clip your Yorkie all over so that his hair is about 1 inch (2.5 cm) long. Trim his ears down to the skin with a trimmer. Trim closer around his anus as well.

WHAT TO ASK A GROOMER

When you first visit your prospective groomer, don't take your dog. Chat with the groomer and ask the following:

1. What are the groomer's qualifications?
2. What experience does she have with Yorkies?
3. Ask whether you can see the facilities and some of the dogs being worked on. The facilities need to be spotless, and the dogs should look calm and well cared for, as well as nicely groomed.

There you have it. A Yorkie can be groomed to a T—at home. With the correct equipment and simple doable techniques, your family pet can look like a real show stopper. Your Yorkshire can really look fancy without a lot of fancy work!

HEALTH OF YOUR
YORKSHIRE TERRIER

There is a current theory floating around that purebred dogs are inherently unhealthy. This is knee-jerk science not based in fact. The truth is, if you want to stack the health deck in your dog's favor, buy him from a breeder who knows her stock, who is an expert in the breed, who tests regularly for known health issues, and who is rigorous in eliminating questionable dogs from the breeding program. Your chances of having a wonderful healthy companion for many years are much better when you buy your Yorkshire Terrier from a reputable, responsible breeder.

The single biggest factor in the health and longevity of your Yorkie is you. Your care and attention, making sure that your Yorkie gets the proper nutrition, sufficient exercise, regular dental care, and good preventive care, will go farther than any other single factor in ensuring that he has a healthy and happy life. And that's the subject of this chapter.

FINDING A VET

One of the first things to put on a to-do list once you have your Yorkie puppy is to find a quality vet. If you are lucky enough to live close to your breeder, ask where the breeder goes or whom she might recommend. If that's not possible, ask friends or neighbors who have small dogs. Yorkies have special needs as far as anesthesia goes, so it's important to find a vet who is experienced with small dogs. Yorkies are so small that a vet unfamiliar with doing surgeries on tiny dogs could incorrectly anesthetize your Yorkie, with disastrous results. Your budget also needs to be considered but shouldn't be the only factor. (And don't consider the most expensive vet as necessarily the best.) Much more important is:

Your potential vet should be compassionate about the health and happiness of your dog.

- **Training:** What is her training? The vet should of course be a graduate of vet school and possibly also have specialty training.
- **Experience:** How long has the vet been in business? Does she see a lot of small dogs in the practice? Vital

is lots of experience with small dogs.

- **Caring:** Is the vet compassionate about the health and happiness of your dog? This is an important criterion for a potential vet.
- **Partnership:** A good vet wants to work with you, being willing to explain diagnoses and procedures fully and to listen to your needs and concerns.

PUPPY POINTER

When you take the time to teach your Yorkie to be a citizen around others, like walking on a leash and sitting when asked, you are not only teaching him good manners but also making it possible for him to be your companion and buddy. Training your puppy well helps him be a happy dog, which may even make him healthier as a result.

THE ANNUAL VET VISIT

Gone are the days of rushing to the vet to get your dog's yearly shots. There has been a revolution in recent years; vet schools, the American Veterinarian Medical Association (AVMA), and the American Veterinary Hospital Association (AVHA) agree: Core vaccinations are generally no longer needed annually.

But your Yorkie does need an annual visit. A yearly vet appointment is essentially a wellness check. It ensures that potential problems get caught early. Small changes in lifestyle can really help your Yorkie live a long and healthy life; your vet will know what these are and how best to implement them.

At the yearly vet exam, the vet will check your dog's heart, look in his eyes, and peer into his ears. She will check his knees for any movement and note any significant difference in his general condition, from his weight to his coat texture. The vet will also perform a heartworm test and check for worms.

WHAT ABOUT PET INSURANCE?

A relative newcomer over the last few years is insurance for your dog. It works like human health insurance, and just as with us, you need to fit the correct plan to you and your Yorkie's needs. Monthly premiums can range between under $10.00 to over $100.00. Be sure to look at plenty of customer reviews for each company you are considering, and read the fine print carefully.

VACCINATIONS

Canine vaccinations have changed the landscape of having a pet so remarkably that most Yorkie owners would not recognize the life and death worries of pet owners as recently as 40 years ago. Vaccinations have ensured that most of the debilitating and fatal diseases that regularly struck down dogs are almost nonexistent today. Today they are still a vital part of canine health.

But like all other medical procedures, vaccinations also carry risk. In recent years, many vets have been concerned with overvaccination. Shots have been given too often and for diseases that most dogs will never be exposed to. Just because "some" vaccinations are vital doesn't mean that "more" are better.

Vaccinations technically don't directly protect the body against a particular disease. They tease it into setting up its own antibodies and protection against the disease, which can take up to 14 days. Vaccinations cause a certain amount of physical stress while doing this. A dog may have mild symptoms of the disease and in some rare cases may develop a full-blown case. That is why it's important to avoid giving your Yorkie vaccinations right before another potentially stressful experience, such as a trip. His immune system will be temporarily lowered by the vaccinations; when added to another activity, they can cause him to become really ill.

WHEN TO VACCINATE

A puppy carries his mother's immunity to disease as long as she is feeding him, so he doesn't need to begin shots until about eight weeks of age. But because it's not known exactly when the mother's antibodies will start to fade and exactly how long the vaccinations will need to create the necessary antibodies in your puppy, he should not have full exposure to the world around him until his full initial series of vaccinations is completed at about four months.

At the other end of the spectrum, your senior Yorkie sometimes doesn't need shots as often as he did when he was a young dog. He is less active and less exposed to potential problems. The inherent stress of the

Younger dogs often need more vaccinations than older ones do.

Vaccinations have ensured that most of the debilitating and fatal diseases that regularly struck down dogs are almost nonexistent today.

vaccinations can harm his older, weaker immune system. Your vet will be able to consult with you on this; some states even allow rabies vaccinations to be waived if a sufficient titer count (that is, the sum of antibodies to a certain disease in the blood) is present.

WHAT TO VACCINATE AGAINST

There are core and noncore vaccines. Core vaccines are essential to the health and life of your dog. Noncore vaccines are either specialized for certain circumstances and so are not necessary for all dogs, or they are limited in their usefulness.

Ron Hines, DVM, PhD, states in the article "What Vaccinations Should My Pet Get?" that the following are core vaccines: distemper (an often fatal viral disease causing high fever and gastrointestinal and respiratory inflammation, sometimes with neurological complications); adenovirus (a family of viruses causing respiratory and gastrointestinal tract infections as well as pink eye); and parvovirus (an often fatal viral disease marked by fever and diarrhea). Three sets of boosters for these vaccines should be given at 7 to 9 weeks, 12 to 13 weeks, and 16 to 18 weeks. Then rabies (a viral disease that is fatal if it reaches the brain) should be given after 16 weeks, with a 3-year booster given the following year. A final vaccination for distemper, adenovirus, and parvovirus should be given sometime after six months and then boosters every three years if the dog is at risk for reinfection. The AVMA recommends that once the core series has been administered, your Yorkie doesn't need to be given the basic vaccinations more than once every three years unless he is in danger of exposure.

Noncore vaccines include those for bordetella (kennel cough), coronavirus (which causes mild gastrointestinal disease), leptospirosis (a bacterial infection

Breeders routinely place their puppies with a spay/neuter contract.

that can pass to humans), and Lyme disease (caused by deer tick bites; it's an acute inflammatory disease characterized by a rash and inflamed joints). How do you determine whether your dog needs these shots? Bordetella is a nonfatal disease that is often passed from dog to dog in close quarters. If your Yorkie attends doggy day care or needs to be boarded while you travel, a bordetella shot can be a good idea. But this vaccine gives immunity only from six months to a year. If you live in an area that is at high risk for coronavirus or Lyme disease, your vet might recommend vaccinating against them. Leptospirosis occurs around stagnant water or after exposure to rodents, so if you don't live on a farm your Yorkie will probably not need a shot for this disease. Also, there have been some studies that the leptospirosis vaccination can cause an allergic reaction. Discuss your options with your veterinarian.

SPAYING AND NEUTERING

Spaying (the removal of the uterus and ovaries of a female dog) or neutering (the removal of the testicles of a male dog) is highly recommended for all pet Yorkies. But he or she should not have the procedure until six and a half months old at the earliest. Anesthesia always carries a certain risk, and Yorkie puppies often have retained canine teeth that need to be surgically removed. So your puppy shouldn't be spayed or neutered until it's clearly evident that there are no retained teeth. That way, the teeth can be taken out at the same time as the spay/neuter surgery, thus avoiding the risk of putting your Yorkie puppy under twice. Tiny Yorkies shouldn't have elective surgery, such as removing canines or spaying/neutering, until fully mature, and such females should have their first season before being spayed. Otherwise they won't be mature enough to handle the surgery.

BENEFITS

Breeders routinely place their puppies with a spay/neuter contract, and puppies adopted from shelters must be spayed or neutered. It's well known in these days of pet overpopulation that it's a good idea to spay or neuter pet dogs.

Males neutered before maturity are far less likely to mark their territory and indulge in other macho behavior. Also, neutering at any age eliminates the possibility of testicular cancer. Females spayed before two and a half years of age have a drastically reduced risk of mammary cancer and of course no risk at all for uterine diseases.

RISKS

What's the downside to spaying or neutering? Number one is surgical risk. Yorkies and other small breeds tend to be much more susceptible to anesthetic complications than their larger cousins. It's definitely a good idea to do this procedure with a vet who is familiar with surgery on small dogs.

Other possible complications aren't as obvious. Reactions to routine vaccinations are more common in altered dogs. Neutering may also increase a male's risk of contracting pancreatitis. There is strong anecdotal evidence that spaying and neutering also increase the tendency toward obesity and urinary incontinence, especially in females.

There are possible hormonal side effects as well, such as hair loss and bone loss, especially when the puppy is spayed or neutered before sexual maturity. In some cases, puppies may never develop a fully adult personality because their actions have never been moderated by the hormonal effects of adulthood. Growth can also be stunted.

BREED-SPECIFIC ILLNESSES

Although the most important factor of a Yorkshire Terrier's health is his owner's care, there are certain conditions you should watch out for. Buying your puppy from a reputable breeder can greatly reduce this risk. Also, make sure to never get a so-called "teacup" or extra-small Yorkie because these dogs are often unhealthy.

Just as certain families get more colds or suffer from allergies, most dog breeds have a tendency to be affected by certain conditions. (By the way, having a "designer" mix doesn't eliminate these tendencies—it just stirs them up.) Reputable breeders watch carefully for these conditions and do their best to eliminate them from their breeding program.

Here are the major breed-specific conditions to watch out for in the Yorkshire Terrier.

BLADDER STONES

If your dog is straining to urinate, has pain when urinating, has bloody or smelly urine, or is having frequent accidents in the house, he may have bladder stones. X-rays or ultrasound will tell for sure.

These stones usually are composed of the chemical compound calcium oxalate and can be formed anywhere in his urinary tract. The condition is generally seen in middle-aged dogs to seniors. Even though some anecdotal genetic predisposition has been reported, there is a strong environmental component to

If your Yorkie appears unusually lethargic, he may be ill and needs to see the vet.

the disease as well. This is yet another reason to feed your Yorkie a good food nutritionally balanced for the breed, as well as plenty of water at all times. Table scraps or a poorly balanced diet, as well as a lack of sufficient water, can contribute to this disease.

BE AWARE!

Repeated vomiting, diarrhea, or overheating can cause dehydration, which can be especially dangerous in a small breed like the Yorkshire Terrier. To tell whether your Yorkie is dehydrated, lift up his upper lip. The gums should be wet, pink, and warm. If they are tacky and pale, he is dehydrated. Give him a drink of water and make sure that he always has access to clean, cool water unless your vet has recommended otherwise. If he is severely dehydrated, he may need intravenous liquids. Consult your vet.

If your Yorkie is diagnosed with bladder stones, he may be put on prescription food (which has a mix of ingredients known to reduce the further growth of stones), or the stones may be surgically removed.

COLLAPSED TRACHEA

A collapsed trachea, or windpipe, basically flattens like a straw that is drawn on too vigorously.

Unlike reverse sneezing (see "Reverse Sneezing" below), a collapsed trachea is less dramatic but more serious. The dog coughs reflexively with a noise resembling a goose honk. If the cough is one or two explosive outbursts and occurs chronically, it's probably a collapsed trachea. The dog coughs to open up his airway.

A collapsed trachea can be treated with anti-inflammatory drugs but often eases with weight loss and the use of a harness rather than a collar, which can compress the airway. A cool mist humidifier and herbal cough remedies can also be used. Supplements that help build cartilage may be helpful as well, as they may at least slow down further deterioration of the airway.

DENTAL DISEASE

Yorkies are very prone to dental disease. This is not just a matter of cosmetics—periodontal disease can lead to cardiopathy, or heart disease. Have your Yorkie's teeth cleaned regularly, and if you can find a vet who does laser teeth cleaning, performed without anesthesia, so much the better.

HYPOGLYCEMIA

Yorkies are so small that they often have difficulty storing sufficient glucose, or sugar. Hypoglycemia, a sudden drop in glucose in a dog's system, can occur in stressed or very active dogs and especially in Yorkie puppies. Puppies are especially susceptible because they have few fat deposits, and the condition may also be connected to an immaturity in liver cells. Symptoms are a sudden loss of coordination, sleepiness, lack of appetite, and general weakness. Left untreated, it can lead to seizures, loss of consciousness, and death.

The magic number concerning hypoglycemia and Yorkie puppies is 2 pounds (1 kg). Until your fully weaned puppy is over 2 pounds (1 kg), he should be fed at least every four hours and be given 1/4 teaspoon of high-calorie paste twice a day.

Unexplained hypoglycemia could be caused by a liver shunt. (See "Liver Shunts" below.)

KERATOCONJUNCTIVITIS SICCA (KVS)

KVS affects many older small dogs, including Yorkies. This can be the consequence of genetics, prescription medications, injuries, or a mix of all three. Basically your dog is not producing enough tears. The eyes will often discharge

Hypoglycemia, a sudden drop in glucose in a dog's system, can occur in stressed or very active dogs.

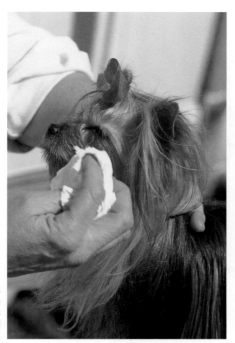

Keratoconjunctivitis sicca is a disease in which the eyes discharge mucus and appear dull.

mucus and appear dull. Unlike PRA (see section "Progressive Retinal Atrophy" below) this is a manageable condition, usually treated with a special salve. If untreated, KVS can cause blindness.

LIVER SHUNTS

In many areas of life, a shunt can be a good thing. With railroad tracks, for example, a shunt bypasses a congested train yard to deliver the passengers to the station swiftly. But when a shunt bypasses a vital body organ, it's trouble. With a liver shunt, the blood is sent around and doesn't flow through the biggest toxin filter in the body: the liver.

Yorkies with liver shunts tend to be small for their age (yet another reason why not to buy a so-called "teacup Yorkshire"). Some other signs are excessive drinking and frequent urination. Shortly after eating, the dog may appear depressed or sleepy, or even have a seizure. These signs are caused by ammonia, a by-product of digestion, reaching the brain instead of being cleared out by the liver.

Prognosis for liver shunts depends on its location, severity, and when it is found. Congenital shunts, which are the kind most common in Yorkies, are good candidates for surgery if diagnosed early. Otherwise the dog must be given drugs that chemically clean the blood.

PATELLAR LUXATION

Patellar luxation, or slipping of the kneecaps, is a difficulty in many breeds under 10 pounds (4.5 kg), including the Yorkshire Terrier. Dislocation can be to various degrees, from 1 (patella slightly loose on the knee) to 5 (permanently dislocated). A reputable breeder will fully disclose the state of your puppy's knees. This is a very manageable condition unless the knees are rated 3 or higher and potentially require surgery. If the puppy has mildly luxating patellas, he can still live a full and healthy life and may be an acceptable choice for a quiet household that doesn't require the dog to do a lot of jumping. Check with your veterinarian for the pros and cons of a Yorkie with this condition moving into your particular living situation.

Vitamin C and glucosamine can help ease the symptoms. Keep your Yorkie lean and give him moderate exercise, especially up gentle hills. Severely luxated patellas require surgery.

PROGRESSIVE RETINAL ATROPHY (PRA)

PRA is a disease in which the dog's retina, which is the lens at the back of the eye, atrophies or degenerates. The dog usually goes blind. It can start when you notice that your Yorkie doesn't see so well at night and then less well during the day too. There is no cure.

Give your dog a weekly health check to help nip potential problems in the bud.

Your chances of PRA in your puppy reduce dramatically when dealing with a breeder who regularly screens the eyes of her stock. Although even quality breeders can find genetic diseases in their stock, they work very hard to breed away from such things—your chances of having a healthy puppy are much higher with a reputable breeder.

REVERSE SNEEZING

Perhaps your puppy has been playing vigorously. He stops, stretches his neck out, splays his front legs, and wheezes heavily. Until you know better, it sounds as if your Yorkie can't breathe. Is this a life and death situation? No, not really.

The condition is called reverse sneezing and requires no veterinary intervention. It is very common in all toy breeds. Basically, the pharynx (back of the throat) goes into spasm, and it calms down in a minute or two. Your Yorkie is not actually having trouble breathing—usually his throat is having spasms because his sinuses are acting up a bit. His mouth will almost always be closed.

An antihistamine can help by opening up his sinuses. Also, try the following to distract your Yorkie:

- Close off his nostrils with your fingers so that he has to breathe through his mouth for a minute.
- Rub his throat.
- Carry him outside.

GENERAL ILLNESSES

Prevention of disease and catching possible difficulties in your Yorkie early is more than just cost effective; it can also mean the difference between having your buddy long into old age or losing him as a relative youngster. Once a week you should check your dog for possible problems, specifically:

- anal region: Check for redness or fecal matter.
- eyes: Check for mucus, redness, or dullness.
- feet: Check for cuts or foreign objects between the pads.
- mammary glands: Check for lumps.
- mouth: Check for pale gums, gum disease and tartar, broken teeth, and bad breath.
- nose: Check for thick discharge.
- penis or vulva: Check for discharge.
- skin: Check for parasites, hair loss, redness, and bumps.
  Consult with your vet if you find anything worrisome.

PARASITE INFESTATIONS

Every Yorkie should be treated for these conditions on a regular preventive basis:

Fleas and Ticks

Aside from the chaos that fleas and ticks can cause in your Yorkie's coat, they are a health menace. Fleas can carry tapeworm larvae and ticks can carry Lyme disease. Treat your dog monthly with a spot-on product, making sure not to bathe him for a week afterward—unlike dogs with a more significant undercoat, it takes that long for the medication to spread all over your Yorkie's skin.

If you notice what looks like little bits of dirt on your Yorkie's skin, it is probably residue left by fleas. You can check for fleas by searching their favorite hideouts: behind the ears, in the armpits, or under the vent. If you find fleas, you can kill them with a good natural flea spray. But if you see one flea, there are probably at

Check your dog for fleas and ticks after he's been playing outside.

least ten others hiding behind nearby hair shafts. A monthly flea preventive will either greatly reduce or entirely eliminate the population.

If you find a tick, don't panic. There are two ways to remove a tick safely. For both methods, don surgical gloves if possible. You don't know whether the tick carries Lyme disease. Also, if you think that the tick might have Lyme disease (because you live around lots of deer or you are in an area where the disease is prevalent), drop it in a jar, close the jar well, and take it to your vet to be checked. Remember that Lyme disease is simple to take care of with a round of antibiotics—*if* you catch it early.

1. **Method 1:** If the tick is in an area where your Yorkie's hair is no longer than 1 or 2 inches (2.5 or 5 cm), you can rub the tick rapidly in a circular motion. After about a minute or two it will back out of your dog's skin and you can dispose of it, preferably down a toilet.

2. **Method 2:** If the tick is attached where your Yorkie has long hair, a rapid circular motion will cause nothing but tangles. Take tweezers, grab hold of the tick as close to the skin as you can manage, and pull it straight out. Then drop the tweezers in alcohol to sterilize them. Dispose of the tick as described above.

Heartworms

These are worms that your Yorkie gets when bitten by a mosquito. The larvae migrate through the blood to the heart, where the worms can grow to an impressive length and eventually shut down the circulatory system. Treatment is draconian and not always effective. Far better is a monthly medication containing ivermectin, which prevents the problem in the first place.

Pinworms, Roundworms, and Whipworms

Pinworms, roundworms, and whipworms are small nematode worms that infest and live off the contents of the intestines and rectum. The Centers for Disease Control and Prevention (CDC) has performed (human) studies on these worms and found that while the populations can greatly be reduced with preventive treatment, they can never be totally eliminated. Such worms bring down the general health of your Yorkie and open him up for other illnesses. Treat on a monthly basis with a fenbendazole product.

DIARRHEA

Diarrhea can happen for lots of reasons, many of them requiring no treatment other than a dose or two of human medication (although check with your vet before dispensing any human medication). Kaopectate, for example, is mild and soothing. But consult your vet if you notice bloody or black diarrhea, diarrhea with vomiting, diarrhea with an elevated temperature, or diarrhea lasting more than a day.

ELEVATED TEMPERATURE

Normal canine temperature is 99.5° to 102.5°F (37.5 to 39°C). If he's excited, a healthy dog's temperature can rise to as high as 103°F (39°C). If the temperature is above 103°F (39°F), call your vet; above 105°F (40.5°C) is an emergency. If it is 98°F (36.5°C) or lower, start warming your dog using blankets that have been warmed in the dryer. Call your vet—below 96°F (35.5°C) is an emergency.

INCREASED APPETITE/THIRST

These conditions are also pretty clear indications that something is wrong. Your vet will be able to discover the cause. Thirst can be the effect of heat but can also be an indicator of several serious medical conditions, such as kidney disease. Increased appetite can be an indicator of diabetes or Cushing's disease.

LETHARGY

If your Yorkie just doesn't seem to have the vigor he once did, and especially if he is eating considerably less, consult your vet. All too often lethargy is considered just one of those things that happens as a dog gets older. This is not necessarily true; it can be linked to a treatable or at least a manageable condition.

VOMITING

Dogs will eat the darnedest things, and the glamorous Yorkie is no exception. This is not a cause for concern unless:

If your Yorkie is out playing in the sun, keep an eye on him to prevent heatstroke.

- the vomitus contains blood (it will look like coffee grounds) or fecal matter
- it's projectile, indicating an obstruction; an obstruction would also be indicated if your dog vomited right after eating
- it's repeated vomiting, which could indicate that your dog has eaten spoiled food or has swallowed indigestible objects; consult your vet if the vomiting continues more than 24 hours, especially if the dog acts depressed or has diarrhea as well
- it's sporadic vomiting, which indicates either worms in the system or a more serious disease; consult your vet if this goes on more than a few days
  Vomiting, especially when accompanied by diarrhea, is the fastest way for a Yorkie to become dehydrated. Your vet may recommend removal of all food to give your dog's system a chance to recuperate. If your Yorkie can't keep down water, he needs to be on IV fluids.

ALTERNATIVE THERAPIES

Although a good vet can be extremely helpful in furthering the health and happiness of your Yorkshire, alternative treatments can complement his care. Your vet may refer you to such practitioners, your breeder may be able to help, or you can look up the major organizations licensing such therapists on the Internet.

ACUPUNCTURE

Acupuncture is the insertion of fine needles in specific areas on the body to balance the flows of energy. This ancient Chinese practice is used to control pain and cure chronic ailments.

CHIROPRACTIC

This therapy is a nonsurgical approach to lameness and spinal disease. Once your vet has ruled out a fracture or tumor, chiropractic can be used as a very gentle means of restoring fluid and nerve flows to an injured area, allowing healing to begin.

HERBAL

Herbal treatments use plant remedies to treat a variety of ailments. For example, alfalfa is used for arthritis and allergies.

HOMEOPATHY

This alternative therapy aims to jumpstart the body's own healing response with very diluted substances that cause the dog's illness. For example, a dog suffering from diarrhea would receive tiny amounts of a substance that causes diarrhea.

FIRST AID

It's great to have veterinary help when you need it, but sometimes there just isn't time. Knowing what to do in an emergency can make the difference between having your Yorkie for many years and mourning his passing tomorrow.

BLEEDING

Bleeding is considered an emergency when it is profuse or the wound is extremely deep. Here's what to do:

- If possible, elevate the wound site and apply a cold pack.
- Cover the wound with a clean dressing and apply gentle pressure to control bleeding.
- Pressure points exist at the inside base of each leg. Applying pressure at these points can slow the flow of blood of the large blood vessels underneath.
- If it is an abdominal wound and organs are exposed, place a warm, wet sterile dressing over any protrusion and cover with a towel. Do not try to push any organs back into the body.
- Allow some bleeding from an animal bite, then clean the wound thoroughly and apply an antibiotic ointment. If very large, the bite will need medical attention.

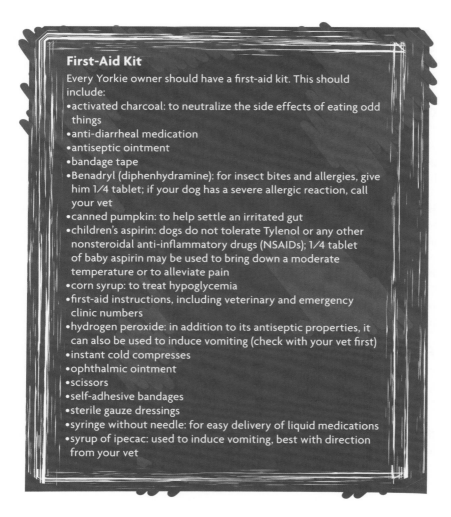

First-Aid Kit

Every Yorkie owner should have a first-aid kit. This should include:

- activated charcoal: to neutralize the side effects of eating odd things
- anti-diarrheal medication
- antiseptic ointment
- bandage tape
- Benadryl (diphenhydramine): for insect bites and allergies, give him 1⁄4 tablet; if your dog has a severe allergic reaction, call your vet
- canned pumpkin: to help settle an irritated gut
- children's aspirin: dogs do not tolerate Tylenol or any other nonsteroidal anti-inflammatory drugs (NSAIDs); 1⁄4 tablet of baby aspirin may be used to bring down a moderate temperature or to alleviate pain
- corn syrup: to treat hypoglycemia
- first-aid instructions, including veterinary and emergency clinic numbers
- hydrogen peroxide: in addition to its antiseptic properties, it can also be used to induce vomiting (check with your vet first)
- instant cold compresses
- ophthalmic ointment
- scissors
- self-adhesive bandages
- sterile gauze dressings
- syringe without needle: for easy delivery of liquid medications
- syrup of ipecac: used to induce vomiting, best with direction from your vet

FRACTURE

Yorkies are sturdy little dogs and don't often have trouble with broken bones. But if your dog is in extreme pain or won't put any weight on a limb, especially if it seems swollen, suspect a fracture. Trying to wrestle a splint onto your dog to immobilize the leg can cause more harm than good. Instead, keep him as quiet as possible, try to cushion the limb from further trauma, and get to your vet right away.

HEATSTROKE

Dogs sweat only through the pads of their feet and so are much more susceptible to the heat than humans are. If you notice that your Yorkie is breathing rapidly and loudly, stop what you are doing. Get him some water and move him out of the sun. If he also has lots of thick saliva and the skin inside his mouth is bright red, he's probably experiencing heatstroke. More advanced signs include high rectal temperature, staggering, diarrhea, coma, and death.

Wet your dog down with cool water and put him in front of a fan. If possible, immerse him in water that is slightly cool but never ice cold. That could result in the constriction of his peripheral blood vessels, making things much worse. Offer small amounts of cool water. Monitor your Yorkie's temperature; when it falls below 103°F (39.5°C), stop cooling him because his temperature will continue to fall. You don't want to cool him too much, as that could present its own set of problems.

Keep a close eye on your Yorkie over the next several days, and don't let him exert himself. Heatstroke can cause lasting effects or even be fatal if you don't allow your dog to recover slowly.

HYPOTHERMIA

Yorkies, with their small body size and lack of undercoat, can have a hard time staying warm in cold weather. If you are walking with your dog for longer than ten minutes in temperatures below freezing, he should wear a coat.

If he starts acting sluggish and "out of it" in the cold, suspect hypothermia. More advanced signs include a body temperature falling below 95°F (35°C), a slowing pulse, labored breathing, and coma.

Warm your dog gradually by wrapping him in a towel that has been warmed in the dryer. Put plastic bottles filled with warm water outside the blankets. You can also put plastic over the blanket, making sure that his head is free. Monitor his temperature and stop warming him when it reaches 101°F (38.5°C). As with heatstroke, don't let your Yorkie exert himself too much for several days after a bout with hypothermia because this could have lasting negative effects.

POISONING

Poisoning can either be a minor matter, something that gives your Yorkie a tummy ache, or life threatening. If you think that your dog has been poisoned, call your vet, or if it's after-hours, call your local emergency clinic or the ASPCA's Animal Poison Control Center: (888) 426-4435. (You will have to pay a consultation fee.)

If your dog comes inside frothing at the mouth as if he's just eaten a bar of soap, assume that he has mouthed or tried to eat some sort of poisonous creature. You must act quickly to stop the toxin from spreading throughout your Yorkie's body. Put him in the kitchen sink and flood his mouth with water from your spray attachment for at least 20 minutes. If not quickly flushed out of his system, the poison will move within minutes through the mucous membranes in your dog's mouth into his bloodstream and throughout his body. Call the ASPCA poison control as soon as possible to confirm your diagnosis, or if there is someone else in the house, have that person call. But flood the dog's mouth with water first.

SENIOR DOGS

One day you look up and your dog has some white in his beard. Yorkies are considered seniors at ten years, although most will probably argue about qualifying for an AARP card.

MAKE ENVIRONMENTAL CHANGES

What changes should you make to his daily routine to keep him happy, healthy, and comfortable in his old age?

A senior Yorkie is more susceptible to heat and cold, so he needs extra protection from both. Also, his skin is more sensitive, so unless his coat can be kept absolutely tangle-free, he should have an easier-care haircut. Senior Yorkies, like all other old dogs, can have trouble hearing and/or seeing. Dogs can adjust remarkably well to such conditions, especially with some extra care from their owners. If you suspect vision impairment, check with your vet to make sure that the condition is not something reversible. Cataracts can be removed.

This is a good point in time to make good on your New Year's resolution to keep a cleaner home; that way there won't be any surprising objects for your Yorkie to trip on. Leave the furniture where it is—if you must rearrange, take him on several tours around the house so that he can get familiar with the new system. If possible, carpet the walkways so that your old boy can easily find his way. You can also put wind chimes or bells on corners so that he can maneuver with certainty.

Hearing can also sometimes be a problem, although Yorkies of all ages can have SHD: selective hearing disability. Dogs with this common "ailment" hear only what they want to hear. Try rattling the food bowl or your car keys; if your old boy doesn't respond, he may be having trouble hearing. After a thorough vet check, you can start teaching him visual commands. With patience and understanding, you really can teach an old dog new tricks!

A senior Yorkie is more susceptible to heat and cold, so he needs extra protection from both.

Senior Yorkies treasure their routine and don't like a lot of change. If changes must occur, respect the right of the old boy to grouse a bit, and be sure to make things as comfortable as possible for him. Games that your Yorkie once loved might now be beyond his abilities, so make sure that children know how to tell when it's okay to play and when he's had enough.

CHECK FOR COMMON SENIOR AILMENTS

Check him out on a regular basis for problems. Don't ever assume that your Yorkie should act a certain way "because he's old." If he is behaving oddly, there is usually a physical reason that can at least be alleviated. The following are some common older dog ailments:

Arthritis

Caused by the degradation of cartilage around the joints, arthritis can result from a specific injury or can just be one of those things connected to the aging process. Symptoms are joint swelling and pain. Conservative treatment involves keeping your Yorkie's weight down, making sure that he has a soft bed, and walking him every other day to keep up mobility. Carpeted stairs to his favorite bed or furniture will also help. Supplements like glucosamine, which stimulate the synthesis of cartilage and chondroitin, help shield cartilage from destructive enzymes and can be effective as well. Your vet can offer prescription drugs, but research them carefully because they often have significant side effects.

Canine Cognitive Dysfunction (CCD)

If your Yorkie is acting as though he doesn't know you or is having trouble remembering important things like the exact location of the treats cabinet, he may be suffering from canine cognitive dysfunction (CCD). This disease is very similar to Alzheimer's in humans. A recent study at the University of California School of Veterinary Medicine states that out of 69 dogs, 32 percent of the 11-year-old dogs and 100 percent of the 16-year-old dogs were affected.

A thorough vet check is in order to rule out other possible problems. Then you will need to reorganize your house to reflect the new reality. Your Yorkie will need to be either under someone's watchful eye or in a safe restricted space behind secure gates. But improvement can come from interesting sources. Teach your old boy a new trick or two—hand signals are fun to learn if his sight is good and will be helpful as he ages. Other possibilities for environmental enrichment include playing with toys or even bringing in another dog to play—or even one to stay.

Diseases like canine cognitive dysfunction (CCD) affect older dogs.

Dog Tale

I first noticed something odd about my dog Robbie's trot when he was a year old. He would walk next to me down the sidewalk with no problem, but as soon as we walked in some grass, his left rear leg would go up and he would start walking on three legs. How strange! After a couple of steps, the offending leg would plop down again as if nothing had happened. I asked my vet about this—she briefly checked Robbie's knees and told me that the left kneecap was a bit loose. I asked her what I should do and she said that sometimes this condition, called patellar luxation, got worse over time, but in mild cases like Robbie's it usually wouldn't. She was right; the condition stayed the same his whole life—even when playing soccer on a big field. I would watch him disappear down toward the end zone with his soccer ball rolling merrily along, then see his little figure go to three legs for a couple of paces and then go back to four again. My funny Robbie!

Dietary changes can also help. Some good ones for CDS contain antioxidants (mixed tocopherols, vitamin C, beta-carotene, carotenoids, and flavonoids), some enzymes, and omega-3 fatty acids (EPA and DHA). In a laboratory study of older dogs over a two-year period, the greatest improvement came from a combination of dietary change and environmental enrichment.

RECOGNIZE WHEN IT'S TIME

There will come a point when whatever old dog disease your Yorkie has will become too much for his system. He will slow way down, stop eating, and lose control of his bladder and bowels. You will probably know when he's ready to go. Euthanasia is a painless release from pain and suffering. Hug your dog, thank him for his many years of companionship, and let him go. You owe him that. A noble and wonderful thing to do in memory of your wonderful dog is to donate in his memory to Yorkshire Terrier Rescue (www.ytca.org), the Yorkshire Terrier Health Foundation, Inc. (www.yorkiefoundation.org), or the American Kennel Club's (AKC) Canine Health Foundation (www.akc.org).

After having had such a wonderful buddy, it can be easy to decide that the pain of losing him makes it just too hard to have another. But the pain will always remain, at least in small measure, until you allow another tiny bundle of cold nose and blue and gold into your life. A new dog—of course a Yorkie—will help more than anything else to bring back the joy of living with this noble breed.

TRAINING YOUR YORKSHIRE TERRIER

Most Yorkshire Terriers see no reason why your job shouldn't be to serve them. To a certain extent, there's nothing wrong with that; it's great to keep your Yorkie's coat flawless, and giving him only the very best is a real pleasure. After all, he is a fancy terrier!

But when well educated, a Yorkie can also make a peerless companion. He needs to (usually) do what you ask, be fully housetrained, and be able to follow simple commands. This requires correct and consistent training.

Whether you do it right or wrong, your dog is always learning from you. If you scream at him when he makes a mess, you are "teaching" him to make messes out of your sight. If you let the neighborhood kids hurt him "by accident," you are teaching him that children are nasty creatures and he should want nothing to do with them. Those examples demonstrate that if you teach your dog an incorrect lesson, you'll have to:

- unteach the wrong lesson
- reteach the correct one

What a lot of work. It's so much easier to take the effort to train your dog correctly the first time.

The most positive and effective training techniques involve doling out treats and praise when your dog does something right.

POSITIVE TRAINING

Just as old-school child rearing used to be "spare the rod and spoil the child," old-time dog training could get pretty fierce. The idea was to dominate your dog to the point where he gave up and listened to you. With the independent, rascally Yorkshire Terrier, that method has never worked. Yorkies need to feel that what you are asking them to do is a great idea and probably theirs all along.

Never consider that yelling is an effective training technique. "That is not negotiable," which can easily be said in a firm, low tone, is very effective, as is a sharp "No!" You can also give your dog a time-out or simply ignore an undesirable behavior. But no yelling, ever (and of course physical punishment is a no-no as well). It's important to realize that dogs are often much smarter than they are given credit for. They know that a sweet, sympathetic voice is often an effort to reassure and ease a worrisome situation, and they know that a loud, angry-sounding voice means that they're being scolded. Far better when training is a calm, self-confident attitude on your part without a whole lot of extra chat. Your Yorkie will sense this and perform more confidently.

The most positive and effective training techniques involve doling out treats and praise when your dog does something right. Treats should be small and yummy, like tiny bits of dog biscuit or hot dog meat.

As you start your training, remember that dogs are not people. They don't think like people. If you try to treat your Yorkie as a small person, your training will fail. Some activities (like barking at the mail carrier, chasing a squirrel, or inviting the neighborhood Shepherd to a takedown) will never stop entirely because they are hardwired into your Yorkie's core. But you can distract him, and sometimes you can even turn his negative action into something positive, like a trick or a training activity.

SOCIALIZATION

Socialization is the act of gradually getting your puppy used to and happy in the big world out there. If you buy your Yorkie as a puppy—at 12 weeks or so—his exposure to other people and especially other dogs needs to be restricted until 2 weeks after his final battery of vaccinations. This would be when he is about 18 weeks or between 4 and 5 months old. Vaccinations take between 7 and 14 days to become effective, and there is no way of knowing exactly when his immunity from disease given to him by his mother will fade. So before four months he is susceptible to diseases such as distemper or parvo and should be a bit sheltered until full immunity kicks in. He shouldn't be interacting directly with strange dogs or walking in parks, and visiting humans should take their shoes off at the door and have clean hands.

HOW TO SOCIALIZE

Does that mean that your Yorkie needs to stay away from all other people and places until then? No.

This is a great time to get him used to riding in the car. Put him in his crate, which should be strapped to the backseat. Go through your bank's drive-through—banks often give dog biscuits. Then on the way home, you can stop off at a quiet sidewalk and practice walking on leash. Praise lavishly!

Have a puppy party—or two. This is a wonderful time to invite people to your home to celebrate your new Yorkie. Just ask that everyone sanitize their hands before patting and take off their shoes. Children can pet too, but they need to sit on the floor before touching the puppy. That way if he wiggles out of their arms he won't fall. This will go a long way toward teaching your independent terrier that strangers can be nice.

Once your puppy has been fully vaccinated, he should meet people and other dogs and visit new places. He can go to the park, hang out with you in your neighborhood, walk around in front of the grocery store—anywhere there are lots of people.

Another great way to socialize puppies once they have had their full battery of vaccinations is puppy kindergarten. In a highly supervised environment your puppy will learn how to interact and behave around lots of other puppies and their owners. Classes are friendly and low key and provide an excellent opportunity for your Yorkie to learn to tolerate other dog breeds. Most quality obedience clubs have such classes; to find one in your area, start at www.akc.org.

CRATE TRAINING

Dogs are hardwired to be den animals. They love tiny enclosed spaces, like under your bed or at the bottom of the sofa cushions. So the "cruelty" and "inhumanity" of a dog crate are really neither. A dog who knows that his crate is a safe space will often want to sleep there even with the door open.

BE AWARE!

Dog parks are a wonderful innovation for many breeds, allowing them to play and exercise around other friendly dogs on a regular basis. Yorkshire Terriers, however, do not generally do well at a dog park, for two reasons.

They are so small that they can be easily bowled over by an overly enthusiastic buddy. Yorkies can also be dog-aggressive, and even the friendliest can suddenly decide that a certain big dog needs to be taken down, with disastrous results.

HOW TO CRATE TRAIN

Most puppies come to their new owner with their crate training already started. But because you will need to continue the training and reinforce it, you need to know all the steps:

1. Put the crate on the floor with the door open, and place a treat for your puppy inside. When he goes to get the treat, praise him. Don't close the door—yet.
2. Take him out to the backyard and play with him until he's really tired, then put him into his crate with a yummy, long-lasting treat.
3. Next put the crate in a quiet room, with the crate door covered with a pillowcase or dish towel. This will signal to your Yorkie that he no longer needs to be a watchdog and can relax.
4. Leave the room. Your puppy will probably sleep now for several hours, then bark or whine to come out. (By the way, when you take your puppy out of the crate after several hours, carry him out to his potty spot. He will be really ready to go!)

5. Puppies make noises so that they can get what they want. They will continue to make the noises you respond to. If your puppy barks when he wants to come out of his crate and you let him out immediately, he will bark more the next time. Instead, tell your puppy "Be quiet for a minute and I will let you out." When he complies, let him out. That way you'll teach him that silence gets him what he wants.

6. At night, exercise your puppy vigorously so that he's really tired. Then put him into his crate. But this time put the crate in your bedroom, next to your bed. If he whines in the night, tell him "Hush." When he quiets, put your fingers into his crate as a reward, and you can both go back to sleep. A 12-week-old puppy should easily be able to hold his bladder all night long.

Obviously a Yorkie who isn't used to a crate or who has been kept crated way too long (more than eight hours) on a regular basis will not enjoy himself there. The way to fix this is to start to feed your puppy in his crate with the door open. Once he has become used to the fact that his crate will not, in fact, bite him, you can shut him in there for a short period. Fun toys, especially the interactive sort that you can stuff with treats or bits of kibble, will help keep him occupied. If he cries, put the crate into another room with a towel over it as necessary. If he's persistent, get earplugs. If you let him out when he cries, you are teaching him to cry and bark to get his way. Do you really want a crying and barking dog?

HOUSETRAINING

Unfortunately, it's very easy to teach your Yorkie puppy to soil your house. All you have to do is let him roam loose. When he needs to go, he'll find a spot he considers suitable. Then it will smell good to him, so he will want to go there again and again. This will not change no matter how much you jump up and down and get angry.

Wee wee pads are an option for a small puppy if you live in a high rise, where it's not always convenient to take your Yorkie out every time he has to go.

Are Yorkies harder to housetrain than other breeds? Not really. Perhaps large breeds are easier to train because they make such big messes that their owners take training very seriously. But if you follow the standard, very simple program outlined here, your Yorkie should be potty trained within several weeks.

HOW TO HOUSETRAIN

Potty training done right is relatively easy.

7. Start with a well-pottied and exercised puppy.
8. Put him into his crate to sleep for three to four hours or for all night, as the case may be. His bladder and rectum will fill but because a dog will naturally not want to mess his bed, he will hold it. When you take him from his crate, go with zero detours outside to his spot. Watch him go and praise, praise, praise.
9. Then bring him in to a somewhat restricted area—for example, put a baby gate across the entrance to the kitchen—and hang out with him. You can put down a newspaper or two just to catch any possible mistakes.
10. After about a half hour to an hour, he will curl up to go to sleep. Then put him back into his crate and repeat the process.

Young puppies should be taken out to potty first thing in the morning, late morning, mid-afternoon, dinnertime, and right before bed, about five times a day. And most puppies need to potty about an hour or two after eating.

Even though the steps are simple, they will take considerable commitment. Now you can see—for the first several weeks your Yorkie puppy will keep you hopping. But done well, housetraining will result in a dog who will never even think of pottying in the wrong place.

HOUSETRAINING ACCIDENTS

What do you do if your Yorkie has an accident? You need to let him know that he did something you didn't like, but yelling will only tell your dog that you are mad and he will just want to get away. A low rumble of a phrase, like "That is not negotiable," is much more effective. Then say "Go potty outside!" and take him out. If he is making puddles when he is behind your back, put him in a belly band (a strip of cloth wrapped around his middle, covering his penis, or if you have a female, in a britches-like diaper), when he is out of your sight. This is not a long-term solution but can be helpful in the interim. If your Yorkie is creating spots around the house that smell good to him, he will return there again and again and it will be essentially impossible to potty train him. But realize as well that if your dog is doing this, you need to restrict his space to where you can keep an eye on him, as you also want to be able to catch him in the act.

BASIC COMMANDS

Basic commands are those things all dogs should be able to do to be able to be a companion and a buddy. All dogs should be able to heel, sit, stay, come, and down.

When training, it is always a good idea to have a bit of motivation along for the ride. Some Yorkies have a favorite squeaky toy, and most enjoy a nibble of this or that yummy treat. (It's always a good idea to train your dog when he is a bit hungry, not right after a big meal, to keep him motivated.) But most of all, your Yorkie wants your praise. While it's not a great idea to yak at your dog constantly during an exercise (it tends to give him the subliminal message that there's something wrong), praise when he's done something right is an excellent educator. At the start you can be lavish with your approval, but over the long haul quiet works best. Most human educators know that a quiet word of approval is much more effective than excessive hooting and hollering, and dogs are no different. When your Yorkie doesn't do something right, simply be silent. Your lack of praise will be an indicator to him that he hasn't responded to your cue properly.

In addition, remember not to say a command over and over. Repeating the command you are giving, as in "Junior, SIT! SIT! SIT! SIT! SIT!" may reassure you but will confuse your Yorkie and make him feel that you don't know what you are doing. (*You* may feel as if you don't know what you are doing, but *he* doesn't have to know.) Give him one command, then gently correct him verbally if he doesn't do it. Your dog will quickly learn that you mean what you say.

A general rule of thumb is that dogs do best with short but frequent training sessions. Sometimes your dog will steadfastly refuse to do what you ask. That's fine. Take him inside and try again tomorrow. Above all, don't rant and rave. Sometimes your Yorkie will absolutely refuse his lesson for several days, then suddenly do it like a champ.

PUPPY POINTER

Puppies are often taught to bark at the door when they need to go potty. To quiet this noise, try this: Buy a jingle bell and attach it to a string. Attach the string to the door you want your puppy to go to when he needs to potty. Make sure that the bell is low enough for him to reach. Each time you open the door for him, jingle the bell a bit and tell him "Go potty! Good boy!" Soon he will associate the sound with going potty, and with a bit of encouragement, will start jingling the bell himself.

HEEL (WALK NICELY ON LEASH)

First, you want your Yorkie to be able to walk comfortably with you on a leash. This can be started quite young, before he has completed his full battery of vaccinations. Just make sure to work in your own yard or on a quiet sidewalk away from most people and dogs.

Walking Yorkies can get a bad rap. They are so easy to pick up and carry that many owners don't bother teaching them how to heel. But if you begin picking up your Yorkie, you'll inadvertently teach him how not to walk on a leash. He'll soon learn that pulling on the leash or refusing to walk will result in a free ride!

When teaching the *heel*, you'll need about a 6-foot (2-m) leash. Don't use a retractable leash for training because you won't have enough control.

How to Teach It

To start, put a comfy chair into your yard, with a good book. Put your Yorkie on his collar and leash. Place him down about 6 feet (2 m) away from the chair, tell him his name and "Let's go!", and then walk over to your chair. Settle into the chair and open to the first page. Your dog will watch you resentfully from the other end of the leash, then eventually decide that it's more fun next to you. When he comes, tell him he is magnificent, wonderful, the best dog ever. Don't do this more than twice the first session.

Once your Yorkie is coming regularly to your chair, carry him about 100 yards (91.5 m) up the road from home. Put him down and tell him "Let's go." Dogs like to go home, so this will encourage him to go with you. As he gets good at this, take him farther away. Then walk him away as well as back home. Soon he will be happily trotting around the block with you.

Now it's time to teach him to heel by your side without pulling on the leash. This is not a stroll. By now your Yorkie probably likes to walk with you. Go fast enough so that he has to work a bit to keep up with you. Go down the middle of a quiet street if possible so that there are fewer side distractions. Pause every once in a while to praise, but again, don't talk constantly because your Yorkie will move away from your side to watch your face. Don't forget, to your Yorkie you are very tall.

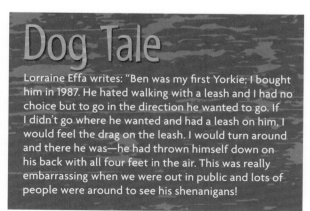

Dog Tale

Lorraine Effa writes: "Ben was my first Yorkie; I bought him in 1987. He hated walking with a leash and I had no choice but to go in the direction he wanted to go. If I didn't go where he wanted and had a leash on him, I would feel the drag on the leash. I would turn around and there he was—he had thrown himself down on his back with all four feet in the air. This was really embarrassing when we were out in public and lots of people were around to see his shenanigans!

The *sit* command is one of the easiest cues for dogs to learn.

Yorkies can go through a clingy stage during leash training in which they try to crawl up your leg or walk under your feet. To deal with this, take a toy or ball with you. Throw the toy or ball and let your dog run out to catch it. This will draw his attention away from you and show him that walking on a leash is not only safe—it's fun!

SIT

Once your Yorkie is happily walking on a leash, you can teach him some other commands. The first is the *sit*. A Yorkie who can sit and watch you can better pay attention and has mastered the first step to the all-important *stay* command.

How to Teach It

Start with your dog on a small stool, on leash. (The stool will restrict his movement a bit, and he will be closer to you.) Stand right in front of him, facing him. Take a small morsel of something yummy, raise it above his eyes and then backward above his head, and say his name and "Sit." The motion will naturally cause him to raise his head and lower his hindquarters to the stool seat. When he moves into a sitting position, reward him immediately with the treat and praise him. Repeat the exercise a couple of times. Doing this 3 to 4 times every day will get better results than trying to do 20 times in one session. If he fights and refuses to comply, stop and try again the next day.

When your Yorkie sits well on the stool, put him onto the ground and do the same exercise.

STAY

Once your dog knows the *sit* you can move on to the *stay*. This command can be particularly difficult for a curious and independent Yorkie. However, when thoroughly taught, it can be hugely helpful. Knowing how to stay, your Yorkie can politely watch you at the dinner table without begging. He can allow guests to come into the house without jumping on their legs with muddy footprints. You can even save his life. For example, if your Yorkie ever gets out the front door and makes a beeline for a busy street full of zooming cars, you can stop him with "Junior! Stay!"

How to Teach It

Have your Yorkie on his leash and collar, directly in front and facing you on a small, steady stool. Tell him his name and "Sit." Then say "Stay!" Wait about a second, then release him with "Good dog!" If you release your dog before he gets the idea to get up and head out, you'll reinforce the command and encourage the general idea that staying is a good thing. Gradually increase the length of the *stay* command; when your Yorkie can do it well for ten seconds, back up a bit. When he can stay like that for ten seconds, back up some more. And so on.

When his *stay* is steady from several feet (m) away, put him onto the ground and repeat the same sequence. Once he can do this, perform the same sequence again but off leash.

COME

Come is another helpful and lifesaving command. For example, if your dog gets loose, yelling "Junior, come!" can be the verbal beacon that brings him home. Of course, your Yorkie already knows this command somewhat—when his dinner bowl jingles, he's probably an expert at swiftly executing the *come*! Teaching the *stay* before this command is important because it allows you some control of the *come*.

How to Teach It

Once your Yorkie is steady on his *stay* on the ground but still on a leash, tell him his name and "Come!" Then back up swiftly. Your curious Yorkie will want to know what you are doing and will follow you. When he does, praise him. As he gets better at this, increase the distance that he has to come. But always keep it fun, short, and sweet. You can always continue the lesson tomorrow.

When your Yorkie is steady on doing this, take the leash off and perform the same exercises again.

Your Yorkie should always feel that coming to you is fun. Never use this command to get your dog so that you can correct him because then he won't want to come anymore. If you need to correct your Yorkie, go to where he is and pick him up. Then tell him firmly in a low voice, "That is not negotiable" and tell him what he did.

DOWN

Once your Yorkie can sit easily, you can teach him the *down*.

How to Teach It

Put him back onto his stool off leash. Tell him his name and say "Down." Put a

A professional trainer can help keep you and your Yorkie motivated and on track.

small goodie in front of his nose. Move it down and forward. His head will follow the goodie, and he should slide into a *down*. When your Yorkie is steady on the stool, teach him the command on the ground.

GETTING PROFESSIONAL HELP

A book can teach you the basics but can't watch you while you train. A live trainer can make suggestions and correct you as you work with your Yorkie. That can be very helpful.

Classes under the care of a good professional trainer can help keep you motivated and on track. There are American Kennel Club (AKC) obedience clubs all over the country; go to www.akc.org to find one near you. The classes are generally inexpensive and can be a lot of fun. If you can't make it to a class or there is nothing near you, you can hire a professional trainer to come to your home. However, these services are considerably more expensive than going to a group class.

You can find a trainer by asking your breeder or dog-owning neighbors for a recommendation. A good trainer should:

- **Be reputable.** Ask for references. The trainer should also belong to some sort of professional organization. The Association of Pet Dog Trainers (APDT) has a user-friendly website at www.apdt.com. You can start your search there.
- **Be knowledgeable.** The trainer should know about the ups and downs of training small terriers. Harsh training methods with Yorkies create nothing but a battleground. A good trainer needs to be skillful, with firm but positive training methods.
- **Have experience.** Ideal is someone who has worked with lots of Yorkies, but if this isn't possible, a good trainer should have lots of experience in working with small dogs.

Your Yorkshire Terrier doesn't need to be perfectly obedient at all times; as an independent terrier, he will sometimes do his own thing. But with these basic skills well learned and well practiced, you can have not only a charismatic charmer but also a companion and buddy who's welcome wherever you go.

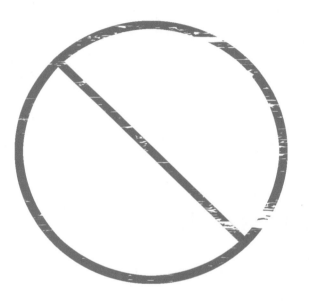

SOLVING PROBLEMS WITH YOUR YORKSHIRE TERRIER

Yorkshire Terriers are cheerful sprites, but they are not always the easiest dogs to live with. Bred originally to be small, independent hunters, their talents don't always fit the modern age of 2.5 children and weekends at the country club. Even when well trained, a Yorkie can make a sudden executive decision to hate your new spouse or decide that the back corner of the living room is a great place to potty. A savvy Yorkie owner knows that she needs some specialized methods to deal with the unique situations the mighty mite can get himself into.

GENERAL PROBLEM SOLVERS

Before we begin talking about specific problem behaviors, here are some great general problem solvers.

THE POWER OF A GOOD YAWN

Yorkies can be excitable creatures. Their terrier heritage dictates that life should be lived in all capitals, so it can be hard to get their attention long enough for them to understand a command. On the other hand, Yorkies sometimes get a glimpse of their actual size in relation to the gargantuan world around them and are too terrified to notice what you are asking them to do.

Dogs are adept at using body language to signal their intentions.

There is a great tool to use in both cases that will generally help your dog be calmer and more attentive: the yawn. When two dogs get together, if one of them starts getting a bit too wild, the other dog will probably slow down, lick his lips a bit, look off to one side, and yawn. It's like secret dog code! The other dog will generally relax. You can do this too. Just slow down, look away a bit, lick your lips, and yawn. This technique works on nervous dogs as well.

LEAVE IT

It can be difficult to teach your Yorkie not to do something. When you tell him that something is wrong or bad, all he knows for sure is that you're cranky right now. Maybe you had a bad day at work—but your dog won't know.

So how do you teach him not to do something? The key is to turn the lesson positive. One way to do that is with *leave it*, a great command for leaving alone dangerous items like exciting cars whizzing past or that shoelace lying on the floor.

Take a small treat that fits in the palm of your hand. Show your dog your hand with the treat firmly hidden in your fist. Tell him "Leave it." Let him sniff and nudge at your hand. When he leaves your hand alone, give him the treat. Repetition is the key here—perform this exercise several times a day. Then off and on, whenever you are playing with your dog and giving him treats, hold one tight in your fist first and tell him "Leave it." When he leaves your hand alone, give him the treat. This will keep the command fresh in his mind. Once he is leaving your hand alone, you can train him to leave alone other things, like smelly socks on the floor or even a dropped chocolate bar.

TOUCH IT

Touch it can be very helpful in gentling a nippy dog. Dogs naturally use their mouths in several ways that people use their hands, like carrying big sticks or telling buddies where to go. But dogs don't always understand that they can't use their teeth on humans as they would on another dog.

Touch it can help with this. Say your dog's name and "Touch it," and invite him to touch your closed hand with a small goodie inside. When he touches your hand, open it and give him the goodie. The idea is for him to not grab at your hand—he gets the goodie only when he touches your hand gently.

THE JOY OF TRICKS

Besides entertaining the neighbors and perhaps the folks at the closest nursing home, tricks can be wonderful tools to solve Yorkshire problem behaviors.

Dog Tale

Yorkie owner Pauline Imbro-Allen writes this tale of a problem-solving Yorkie.

"We lived in a neighborhood with sidewalks and curbs. It had been snowing and we plowed out the driveway and the front walkways. Nugget was outside, and she spotted my daughter walking back to the house and took off to meet her. Instead of going around the driveway and front walk, the clear path, she decided to run across the lawn. She jumped onto the snow and sank—all you could see was the top of her back and her head and tail sticking up. If you watched her you could tell she was still running her little feet but realized she was getting nowhere. We pulled her out and from that day on she never jumped onto the snow again. She knew to test it each and every time after that experience."

Yorkshire Terriers will chase small quick-moving creatures and can be very protective. They are hardwired to be independent thinkers, so they don't ask your permission before chasing down the small child who is screeching down your hallway. You can't "teach" them to not do this. Yes, basic obedience really helps and plenty of exercise is a must. But knowing a trick or two can be a godsend. If you can distract your Yorkie's attention with something else that he really likes to do at the moment when he is about to do something inappropriate, you can break the cycle of must-chase-small-child or whatever the situation is.

Teaching your Yorkie a trick is easy. First watch him in action—dogs naturally perform cute behaviors all day long. When you see your Yorkie do something cute, name the action. Then every time he naturally does the trick, say the name out loud and reward him with a treat. Sooner or later your Yorkie will connect the action to the name and treat. Soon you will be able to say the name of the trick and he will perform it on command.

PROBLEM BEHAVIORS

Sometimes things go great—and sometimes they don't. When your Yorkie has a specific problem behavior, you need specific directions on what to do about it.

HELP! MY YORKIE WON'T STOP BARKING!

Yorkies are surprisingly quiet—for a terrier. This is because they are "mousers" as opposed to "ratters." Ratters, such as Jack Russell Terriers and Border Terriers, bark at their prey; mousers stare their prey down, and then when the target moves,

Sometimes puppies can go through a chewing phase, which can become permanent if not nipped in the bud.

they pounce. But a Yorkie takes his job as protector of hearth and home very seriously. Part of this can be warning intruders or barking at the four corners of the backyard. Fortunately, several tools can be helpful in keeping the noise level down.

If there are a lot of people moving in and out of the house for a limited period, it's probably a good idea to put your Yorkie into his crate and cover the door with a sheet or a pillowcase until things quiet down. This is the signal that your mini doorbell can relax and go off duty.

The best way to teach your Yorkie to stop barking is to teach him how to bark. Basically, if you can gain control at the start of the action, you can end it too. Here's how to do it:

1. When your Yorkie barks (at a point in time when it's okay), say his name and "Bark! Good dog!"
2. When he barks on command and only then, say "No bark! Good dog!" Reward him with a treat the instant he stops barking.
3. The next time he barks when you'd like him to stop, say "No bark! Good dog!" He should now cease barking because he has been taught to anticipate a reward for stopping the barking.

HELP! MY YORKIE IS CHEWING!

Yorkies are not generally big-time chewers. But sometimes puppies go through phases of this, which can become permanent if not nipped in the bud. In fact, they sometimes enjoy chewing on things as their molars appear, at 8 to 12 months of age. They may decide that table legs or electrical cords are especially yummy.

Products are available to put on furniture or electrical cords that are harmless but taste horrible to a dog. You can make a product like this at home too by mixing petroleum jelly with generous amounts of cayenne pepper. (This is safe to put on furniture.) Your puppy will try the object once and never go back to it again. You should also ramp up the stuff your puppy can chew. For example, there is no better chew toy to a Yorkie than a raw bone, which you can find at the grocery store. The more chew toys your Yorkie has, the less likely he will be to munch on inappropriate or dangerous items.

HELP! MY YORKIE IS DIGGING!

Yorkies aren't really prone to digging, but every once in a while a Yorkie will decide that your landscaping is inadequate to his needs and take matters into his own hands. The solution is rather simple. When you notice a hole, put a roll of his stool in the bottom. When your Yorkie goes back to expand on his work, he will quickly decide that he doesn't want to dig there anymore after all. Once you've done this several times, he will look for a different pastime.

Usually a persistent digger needs more exercise and is just bored. You can supply a digger with toys that supply long-lasting fun like a ball that if rolled just right drops a piece of kibble.

HELP! MY YORKIE ESCAPES OUT THE FRONT DOOR!

Yorkies aren't usually escape artists, but you can't overestimate the deep panic that chews your gut when your dog runs loose out of the house. All dogs need to learn basic good manners at the front door.

First, make sure that he is well versed and steady on his *sit* and *stay* commands. Your Yorkie needs to know that he never goes in front of a human through a doorway. This includes inside the house. To teach him this:

1. Sit your Yorkie next to you at the door.
2. Tell him "Stay!"
3. Move ahead of him through the door.
4. Release him with the command "Let's go!" and let him move through the door.

If you have more than one person in your household, one person needs to do the basic training but everyone needs to know the commands and use them.

A tight lead may stress your dog when you take him out to potty.

After all, what good is it if your dog listens to you but is willing to run between the legs of your five-year-old?

HELP! MY YORKIE FORGOT HIS HOUSETRAINING!
It's actually pretty easy to potty train a Yorkshire if you are consistent. But what do you do if you're having trouble? Or what happens if your Yorkie backslides? There are two areas that can be particularly troublesome.

My Yorkie Won't Potty on Lead
Your Yorkie sniffs and sniffs until you feel he knows every blade of grass on a personal basis, yet he won't go. Then you decide that he doesn't really need to go, you come back inside, and—boom—he does his business right there. Why does he do that?

It's important to realize how much you communicate to your dog through his leash. If the leash is tight or you are jerking him from place to place, you are not helping matters. Most of us like to do our business in a quiet, unstressed environment. So do our dogs.

So first and foremost, loosen up. Loosen your hand on the lead. Go to where you want your dog to go. Stop. Become a post. Let your dog walk around you, finding the right spot. Watch the pretty clouds or an interesting tree. Pretty soon, if he needs to go, he will squat. Once he does, praise him enthusiastically.

Continue this until your dog appears to be done. Then take a nice walk. You don't want to head straight back to the door as soon as he's done because that tells him that the longer he holds it, the longer the walk will be.

If you follow these steps, pottying on a leash can become a regular and happy routine.

My Yorkie Potties in the House

If your Yorkie is still pottying in the house even after following the steps outlined above, take him for longer walks. When you get back home, put him into his crate and then take him out to potty again after about half an hour. When you are not home your dog should be in his crate, although an adult should be crated no more than eight hours at the most.

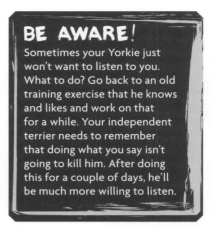

BE AWARE!
Sometimes your Yorkie just won't want to listen to you. What to do? Go back to an old training exercise that he knows and likes and work on that for a while. Your independent terrier needs to remember that doing what you say isn't going to kill him. After doing this for a couple of days, he'll be much more willing to listen.

When your boy is out and about in the house, he should either be in a restricted area of the house or in a belly band. This is a cloth strip with Velcro strips on each end, wrapped around your Yorkie boy's middle, covering his penis. You can put a panty liner at the appropriate spot if you'd like as reinforcement. Have a drippy girl? Use a britches intended for females in season.

Then do a super house cleaning, getting in every single little corner, with the goal of really eliminating the smell. Even when everything smells great to you, your dog will still be able to hone in on that "good-smelling" spot. Use enzymatic cleansers specially formulated to remove the urine scent. If you have been thinking about changing your carpet, now would be a good time to do so. Your goal is to eradicate every single "yummy-smelling" spot in your house.

Every time you catch your boy lifting his leg (or your girl squatting) in the house, give a sharp "Ahhh!" and tell him in a low, firm tone, "That is not negotiable." Then take him outside to potty. You should tell him "Potty OUTSIDE!" but you don't need to yell so much as really show him what he should do. Neutering will moderate the leg lifting in your boy and should help with the sniffing, but this is primarily a behavior issue, and behavior modification is what will take care of it. Unfortunately, spaying doesn't make any difference to the behavior of a female.

Pottying in Winter

Yorkshire Terriers, due to their small body size and lack of undercoat, can be more susceptible to the cold than many other breeds. Sometimes they simply won't potty outside. When it's cold, rainy, or snowy it can be much easier to find a spot in your nice warm house and put up an exercise pen with lots of newspapers. You can hang out with your Yorkie so that he's not lonely. You will have some cleanup to do, but it will at least be in an area you designate.

HELP! MY YORKIE IS A POGO STICK!

Although a Yorkie won't generally topple a child by jumping up on her, a dog who mimics a pogo stick can only be annoying, especially when greeting guests.

In some circumstances a great jumping dog can be an absolute asset. Yorkies who participate in obedience or agility, for example, certainly need to be able to joyously bound from place to place. But there is a time and a place for jumping. At the front door, no one wants to be bowled over by a whirling dervish.

When teaching your dog not to jump up, everyone in your family needs to be willing to work with your pogo stick. One adult who secretly thinks that Junior is

Everyone in the family must commit to teaching your Yorkie not to jump up.

cute when he jumps up on guests will wreck your plan, so make sure that everyone is on board.

First you need to teach your Yorkie how to sit as outlined in Chapter 7. Dogs learn best with short, frequent training sessions, so over several days lengthen the length of the *sit* to about three minutes. Then make sure that your boy can sit for three minutes without the leash.

Next have a friend come over to help. Ask the friend to come to the door and knock softly. Tell your dog, now back on the leash, "Sit." Your friend shouldn't even come in the front door until he is steady on his *sit*. Once he is steady with the knocking, your friend can come inside and should be able to say a friendly hello to you without Junior attacking her with joyful bouncing. So very important when your friend comes in is to *ignore the dog*.

When your boy is steady on his *sit*, even after your friend has greeted you and chatted for a moment, she should reach down and give the dog a pat. You can release your Yorkie with "Say hello" or even "Give paw" if he has learned this trick. He will be rewarded for being quiet and respectful by the attention your friend showers on him; this will encourage him to be quiet and respectful even more. You are done when your Yorkie is steady on this step, doing it several times over several days.

HELP! MY DOG HATES MY SPOUSE!

Sometimes the bond with a Yorkie is stronger with a husband than the wife—or vice versa. This can lead to difficulties and frustration for everyone involved. The solution lies in having the disliked spouse proving to your Yorkie that she is the prime source of the good stuff.

Your wife (if she is the disliked one) needs to be the only one feeding the dog, including treats. When she comes into the room she should ignore your Yorkie but occasionally drop bits of goodies for him to eat. When your wife sits down to watch television or eat supper, she should ignore your Yorkie but occasionally throw goodies on the floor for him. If and when your dog comes up to her for more, she should give your Yorkie a goodie and praise him.

Your dog won't change his attitude overnight, but hopefully these tactics will help!

GETTING PROFESSIONAL HELP

The definition of insanity is to continue to do something despite the fact that it's not working, in a vague hope that continued efforts will produce results. So if you are working with your Yorkie on some training activity and you aren't getting anywhere in a reasonable timeframe, change tactics. Do this in a two-step approach.

1. Look back at the original book or go back to the person from whom you got the training idea. The question to ask yourself is: "Am I doing this right?"

Some problem behaviors may require professional help.

2. If you were doing things correctly and it's not working, it's time to change gears.

If you have changed your gears several times without success, it's time to get help. Your breeder can often give advice, or sometimes books and websites have tips that make all the difference.

But when that isn't enough, you need to find a professional. Many vets have a behaviorist on staff. Also, if you go to obedience classes, your club may be able to recommend a good professional.

A good behaviorist:

- has experience and a track record of successfully working with dogs, especially small dogs
- can get inside your Yorkie's head and can see how he ticks—that's often the key to success
- is not slavishly married to any one training method, as long as it is kind
- is willing to listen and work with you; after all, you know more about your Yorkie than anyone else

Owners drop their dogs off at shelters every day because they were unable to resolve some training issue with their dog. When you've tried everything and it's not good enough, be smart and get professional assistance.

PUPPY POINTER

It can be argued that Yorkie puppies are the cutest of all dogs. Those eyes! The fluffy puppy hair! But supreme cuteness can be a major training deterrent. Your puppy may be able to get away with behavior that would never be tolerated in a less darling dog. Then, by the time that the nipping or little puddles aren't so adorable, the behavior has become a habit and is much harder to eradicate. Treat your little precious with kind firmness from the start and you will have a much easier time of it.

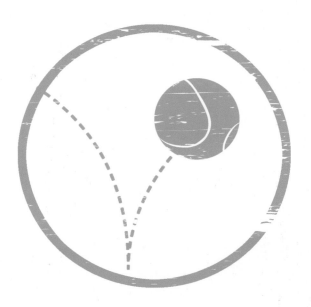

ACTIVITIES WITH YOUR
YORKSHIRE TERRIER

The Yorkie was made to be an out-and-about dog. Independent and confident, a Yorkie likes to hang out with you, whether you are competing together, doing therapy work, or heading cross country. Yorkies were never made to wait patiently for you to arrive back from the business of life. They want to be in the thick of things.

SPORTS AND ACTIVITIES

Yorkshire Terriers are well suited for a surprising variety of canine sports. Beneath the flowing mantle of blue and gold lies the heart of an independent hunter, athletic and able to zig and zag after the fleetest of small creatures. Besides, a Yorkie's greatest desire is to hang with his owner. He will enjoy any sport that requires working closely with you.

AGILITY

If your phys ed program in school ever included an obstacle course, you have a good idea of what canine agility is. As is required in some human courses, dogs go through tunnels, negotiate weave poles, walk a balance beam, and perform other feats, all as fast as possible. Precision isn't as important as swiftness, which is great for Yorkies, as a picture-perfect straight *sit* is not their strong point. If well done,

The fast and nimble Yorkie excels in the sport of agility.

It is tempting to try every training idea right away with your Yorkie puppy. But puppies need to have full vaccine immunity, usually at about four months, before they should hang around other dogs. They shouldn't attend any formal classes before then. At about four months, they are much better off working with you on their basic obedience and housetraining at home while attending a puppy kindergarten class. At about six months, they can begin basic obedience and/or conformation classes.

Due to the amount of jumping involved, Yorkie puppies should not start agility until they are fully mature at about one year of age.

everyone in agility just has a rollicking good time. Because this sport requires jumping, check with your vet that your Yorkie's knees are absolutely sound. You will be running alongside your dog shouting encouragement, so you'll need to be in good shape as well.

CANINE FREESTYLE

Canine freestyle has been referred to as dancing with dogs, but it is more like a beautifully scripted ballet in which one of the participants happens to be canine. Canine freestyle is difficult for most Yorkshire Terriers. They are so small that it is hard for them to catch their partner's nonverbal commands, and they lack the extreme discipline to drill in a performance over and over until it is pitch perfect. There are always exceptions to any rule, but in general, this is not a great sport for Yorkies.

CANINE GOOD CITIZEN TEST

The American Kennel Club's (AKC) Canine Good Citizen program is something in which all Yorkies can and should participate. The CGC takes the basic good manners necessary for canine companionship and turns them into a test with a prize at the end. Your Yorkie will need to pass the following:

1. accepting a friendly stranger
2. sitting politely for petting
3. appearance and grooming
4. out for a walk on a loose leash
5. walking through a crowd
6. sitting on command

7. coming when called
8. reaction to another dog
9. reaction to distraction
10. supervised separation

When your Yorkie passes all ten tests (often administered at dog shows), he will receive a certificate and can proudly add the initials "CGC" after his name. And the fact that he now has the good manners necessary to be a most excellent companion is much more than just the icing on the cake.

CONFORMATION

Conformation is a sport that helps breeders sort out and identify their best stock to continue to future generations. Every dog breed has a list of ideal attributes, called a standard. The Yorkie standard talks about correct Yorkie temperament, goes over body proportions, describes what a perfect headpiece should be, and speaks in great detail about the ideal Yorkshire coat. The closer a particular Yorkshire Terrier approximates this standard, the better he will do in conformation.

If you watch a dog show on television and think that it looks like a bunch of people milling about and hanging out with their dogs—think again. This is a sport similar to dressage in horses, where ideally the handler fades to invisibility and the animal just looks amazing. A properly shown Yorkie with his coat rippling like a deep silver waterfall can take your breath away.

Owner Pauline Imbro-Allen writes about her Yorkie McNugget:

"McNugget and I decided to do an obedience class at a local vo-tech school. We bonded and were having fun together. We continued our training and went on to earn our Companion Dog (CD) and Companion Dog Excellent (CDX), and then one day we were in Utility. She qualified that day with a 170.5 score (170 is passing) because she decided she didn't want to sit. She was one of four dogs who passed, and I was so proud of her that it didn't matter what her score was. She made it through all the stresses and completed her first leg in Utility!"

If you think that you might like to show your Yorkie, speak to your breeder and attend local dog shows. Go to www.infodog.com for more details. Ask around ringside or go to the AKC's site at www.akc.org for available clubs and classes.

OBEDIENCE

Obedience is a sport wherein a dog and trainer perform certain precise exercises while being judged on correctness and accuracy. At the CD level, the dog is required to heel quickly or slowly, on or off lead as the judge requires, stand for examination, sit quietly with the owner across the ring, and do likewise for a *down* of several minutes. CDX is off-lead heeling only and adds directed jumps. The UD level adds scent discrimination.

Yorkies can do surprisingly well in obedience, and several have achieved top honors. They do require a handler who understands a terrier's need for variety and fun in training.

RALLY

In this sport, a course is set up with a series of signboards in the ring; dog and handler move from one numbered sign to the next on the course, performing each as directed. The exercises are very similar to those required in regular obedience.

Yorkies can do as well in rally as they do in obedience, although rally does require that the handler can read and follow directions well. This can be easier said than done; if you have trouble being the navigator on a road trip, you might want to skip rally.

THERAPY WORK

The job of a therapy dog is to be friendly and give comfort to people in hospitals, retirement homes, schools, and in stressful situations such as disaster areas. Therapy dogs collect pats and hugs and sit on laps; some can even perform simple tricks. Their overall job is to brighten a person's day. Therapy dogs have been proven to help healing in hospitals, successfully reach out to children having trouble in school, and ease stress in disaster zones. Well-socialized and well-trained Yorkies make excellent therapy dogs. They have a magic trick—their "awww" factor can melt the most frozen heart.

During World War II, Corporal William Wynne was given a Yorkie abandoned on a New Guinean battleground and named her Smokey. When Bill was hospitalized, his army buddies smuggled Smokey in to cheer him up. Using her native Yorkie charm, Smokey immediately became a hit with everyone in the ward. When the commanding officer, Dr. Charles Mayo (of the Mayo Clinic), discovered the subterfuge, he allowed Smokey to stay at the hospital if she earned her pay; she went on rounds, cheering up the other wounded soldiers and was allowed to sleep with Bill at night. So the first known therapy dog was a Yorkie!

Well-socialized and well-trained Yorkies make excellent therapy dogs.

The Delta Society, one of several organizations that certifies and registers therapy dogs, has a four-step program for interested applicants:
1. Take a training course—that's for you, not your dog.
2. Get a vet check.
3. Get evaluated as a team.
4. Submit an application.

Yorkies can often reach patients who find larger dogs intimidating. Being a therapy team can be very rewarding work for both you and your dog.

TRAVELING WITH YOUR YORKIE

Small enough to fit anywhere yet with a bright, inquisitive personality, there is no better traveling companion than the Yorkshire Terrier. Yorkies can turn a ho-hum "Are we there yet?" trip into an adventure. If you use the correct equipment and follow the canine rules of the road, the two of you will be unstoppable.

Never travel with your Yorkie, even for an afternoon, without bringing along a sturdy leash and collar. He will occasionally need to put all four on the floor if only to go potty.

Here is some equipment that can make your trip smooth sailing:
- enough food for the trip
- favorite dog toys
- first-aid kit
- hard-sided plastic crate
- large carrying purse
- poop bags
- soft-sided triangular carrier with wheels
- walking leash and collar
- water, either bottled or from home

TRAVELING BY AIR

Flying with your dog certainly is the most rapid way to move from Point A to Point B. Yorkies fly especially well in the cabin, under the seat in front of you.

A triangular soft-sided carrier, especially one with wheels, is the best way to go. Yes, a determined small dog can try to chew or bite his way through cloth and mesh. If you try putting your Yorkie into his carrier—well in advance of your trip, of course—and he acts like a lifer trying to escape from Alcatraz, he needs a review of basic crate training. (See Chapter 7.) A soft-sided carrier has plenty of airflow with lots of mesh siding so that your dog can breathe easily. The triangular shape of this carrier means that when it is upright, he can sit up fully. When you lay it on its side, like under the airline seat in front of you, he can stretch out almost completely. It has a telescoping handle and wheels so that you can pull it behind you and straps so that you can also use it as a backpack.

You'll want to bring a hard-sided plastic crate with you as well. You can pack it as one of your suitcases. Your Yorkie will need the security of a regular crate at your destination. The best plastic crates have dials to hold the top and bottom together.

Airlines generally don't require travel health certificates for dogs flying in

Dog Water

After two to three days of travel, it's usual for most dogs to have loose stools. This is caused by drinking water they aren't used to and can be alleviated by making sure that your Yorkie drinks only water from home. Bring 1 or 2 gallons (4 or 7.5 l) of water with you if you are traveling by car, or just use bottled water.

the cabin. But certainly double-check to make sure. When you make your airline reservation, say that you want to bring your dog with you. The agent will go over the exact requirements. You must make a reservation for your Yorkie as well as for you; although you generally won't have to pay for him until you check in, most airlines have a limit of two dogs in-cabin per flight. If you plan to change flights, make sure that all the airplanes you want to use can accommodate in-cabin dogs. Some planes are just too small. Also, if you are traveling overseas, your arrival country will certainly want a health certificate and may have other stringent requirements. Check the country's website for more information.

Obviously you should arrive early to check in with your Yorkie. And security will want to check out the in-cabin bag while you carry him through the metal detector. A small note here: Although you pay a handsome extra fee to bring your dog in-cabin, the airplane considers him one of your carry-on bags. Unfair but true!

Most airlines will let people who need a bit of extra time board early. It's smart to take advantage of this. Once you are at your seat, settle your Yorkie in and then leave him alone. The more you talk to your dog, pat him, reassure him, and reassure yourself that he is all right, the more you're actually telling him that there is something to worry about. Enjoy your magazine and the view above the clouds. Your Yorkie may be restless for a bit, but when he can tell that you are unconcerned he will calmly fall asleep.

BE AWARE!

It can happen in a second: The door was left ajar and your Yorkie disappeared. He is microchipped and has his collar on, including his rabies tags, but of course now is not the time to sit back and hope that you will get lucky. Time is of the essence. If you notice that your dog is gone within a couple of minutes, he probably hasn't gotten that far. Get out there and call your dog.

Plan A: He's gotten farther away, by himself, than he's ever been. He's not so sure of himself. So if your Yorkie sees you and you try to pounce on him, you will probably scare him. He may run, and even a small Yorkie can get away in a fashion that no human can follow. Calmly tell your Yorkie to stay, and go over and pick him up. If you had enough presence of mind to pick up some food as you pelted out of the house, show him what you have and approach slowly. If you have nerves of steel, make sure that your Yorkie can see you and then you run away, as if playing a game. He will likely follow you.

Plan B: If you've run out of the house, called and called your Yorkie, and he is still nowhere to be found, Plan B may help. Every Yorkie owner should have at least 20 lost dog posters made up and ready to go. The posters should be on either 9 x 14 or 11 x 17 paper. Each poster should contain:

- A large picture of a Yorkie with a very large "LOST DOG" headline. Remember that most people will see the poster from their car.
- The fact that your dog is microchipped and needs medication. This lets anyone who might have picked up your Yorkie know that you can positively identify the dog as yours and that he may need extensive and expensive medical care. They don't need to know that the "medication" is your Yorkie's monthly heartworm preventive.
- Your telephone phone number so that you can easily be reached should someone locate your dog.

If your Yorkie is lost during the day, try to get these posters out within the hour. If lost at night, try to have them out by first daylight. Then fax the posters to all of the local vets in your area. Call your local animal control to let the staff know what's going on, and follow their instructions. Call the local police as well—some will accept lost dog data. Follow up every couple of days.

TRAVELING BY CAR

If you have taken your Yorkie puppy in the car to lots of fun walks and visits, he should enjoy riding in the car. If for some reason he doesn't, take it slowly. Sit with your Yorkie in your parked car for a couple of minutes a couple of times a day until he relaxes—and don't forget to treat him at the same time. Then take a turn around the block. Continue going on longer and longer rides to fun places like the dog park until he is comfortable in the car.

When traveling by car, your Yorkie should be securely fastened in the backseat.

Just as you would never allow your children to ride in a car other than in the backseat with their seat belt securely fastened, your Yorkie needs to be securely fastened in the backseat as well. You can keep him in his hard plastic crate and belt it in, or you can use his soft carrier, also securely belted in. The top of the carrier can be unzipped if your Yorkie is snapped into the carrier's tether. There are also doggy car seats on the market.

Settle your dog into his crate or carrier, put some music on, and off you go. Let him know by your calm attitude that everything is okay and he will quickly curl up and fall asleep. Stop once every two or three hours for a potty break. It will do you good to stretch your legs as well!

PET-FRIENDLY LODGING

In the past, most hotels felt that allowing dogs in their rooms wasn't worth the potential mess and damage. But as more and more of the dog-owning public is traveling with its animals, many hotels have changed their minds. Sometimes luxury hotels even have a separate canine menu. Be sure to ask before you make your reservation whether your hotel allows dogs. Some charge a bit extra for this privilege.

Once there, it's important to treat your hotel room with the utmost respect. Remember that you are an ambassador for every dog-owning traveler who follows you; how you and your dog behave will affect the management's decisions about all canines in the future. Unfortunately, it takes only one badly behaved dog to sour management on all doggy guests. Make sure that your Yorkie isn't that one dog! Follow the following rules scrupulously:

- Always pick up after your dog, and potty him only in the hotel's designated areas.
- Unless you are absolutely 100 percent sure that your Yorkie will not potty in the hotel room, keep him in his crate at all times in the room. If loose, have him or her only in a belly band (male) or britches (female). Many dogs who are absolutely clean at home are not so on the road because their schedule has been changed.
- Carry your Yorkie through all public areas. Even the best-mannered dog can make a mistake in a strange place. Once they need to go, most dogs are not used to walking for several minutes before they can relieve themselves.
- If you must leave him alone in the room, keep him in his crate with the door covered, as this will show your dog that he is off duty and can relax. If your Yorkie insists on barking, you will need to respect the other guests and take hiim with you. Perhaps the concierge can hook you up with a local doggy day care where you can leave your Yorkie for a few hours.

Your Yorkie can be your companion, buddy, and partner in adventure. Most Yorkie owners, once smitten, swear they will never have another breed. Forged in the Yorkshire hills as a tough and independent hunter, refined in English drawing rooms as the original fancy terrier, the beautiful Yorkie wakes up every day cheerful and contemplating his next mischief. How bad can life be if you are owned by a Yorkshire Terrier? Not bad at all.

RESOURCES

ASSOCIATIONS AND ORGANIZATIONS

BREED CLUBS

American Kennel Club (AKC)
5580 Centerview Drive
Raleigh, NC 27606
Telephone: (919) 233-9767
Fax: (919) 233-3627
E-Mail: info@akc.org
www.akc.org

Canadian Kennel Club (CKC)
89 Skyway Avenue, Suite 100
Etobicoke, Ontario M9W 6R4
Telephone: (416) 675-5511
Fax: (416) 675-6506
E-Mail: information@ckc.ca
www.ckc.ca

The Canadian Yorkshire Terrier Association (CYTA)
www.cyta.ca

Federation Cynologique Internationale (FCI)
Secretariat General de la FCI
Place Albert 1er, 13
B – 6530 Thuin
Belqique
www.fci.be

The Kennel Club
1 Clarges Street
London
W1J 8AB
Telephone: 0870 606 6750
Fax: 0207 518 1058
www.the-kennel-club.org.uk

United Kennel Club (UKC)
100 E. Kilgore Road
Kalamazoo, MI 49002-5584
Telephone: (269) 343-9020
Fax: (269) 343-7037
E-Mail: pbickell@ukcdogs.com
www.ukcdogs.com

Yorkshire Terrier Club of America (YTCA)
www.ytca.org

PET SITTERS

National Association of Professional Pet Sitters
15000 Commerce Parkway, Suite C
Mt. Laurel, New Jersey 08054
Telephone: (856) 439-0324
Fax: (856) 439-0525
E-Mail: napps@ahint.com
www.petsitters.org

Pet Sitters International
201 East King Street
King, NC 27021-9161
Telephone: (336) 983-9222
Fax: (336) 983-5266
E-Mail: info@petsit.com
www.petsit.com

RESCUE ORGANIZATIONS AND ANIMAL WELFARE GROUPS

American Humane Association (AHA)
63 Inverness Drive East
Englewood, CO 80112
Telephone: (303) 792-9900
Fax: 792-5333
www.americanhumane.org

American Society for the Prevention of Cruelty to Animals (ASPCA)
424 E. 92nd Street
New York, NY 10128-6804
Telephone: (212) 876-7700
www.aspca.org

The Humane Society of the United States (HSUS)
2100 L Street, NW
Washington DC 20037
Telephone: (202) 452-1100
www.hsus.org

Royal Society for the Prevention of Cruelty to Animals (RSPCA)
RSPCA Enquiries Service
Wilberforce Way, Southwater,
Horsham, West Sussex RH13 9RS
United Kingdom
Telephone: 0870 3335 999
Fax: 0870 7530 284
www.rspca.org.uk

SPORTS

International Agility Link (IAL)
Global Administrator: Steve Drinkwater
E-Mail: yunde@powerup.au
www.agilityclick.com/~ial

The World Canine Freestyle Organization, Inc.
P.O. Box 350122
Brooklyn, NY 11235
Telephone: (718) 332-8336
Fax: (718) 646-2686
E-Mail: WCFODOGS@aol.com
www.worldcaninefreestyle.org

THERAPY

Delta Society
875 124th Ave, NE, Suite 101
Bellevue, WA 98005
Telephone: (425) 679-5500
Fax: (425) 679-5539
E-Mail: info@DeltaSociety.org
www.deltasociety.org

Therapy Dogs Inc.
P.O. Box 20227
Cheyenne WY 82003
Telephone: (877) 843-7364
Fax: (307) 638-2079
E-Mail: therapydogsinc@
qwestoffice.net
www.therapydogs.com

Therapy Dogs International (TDI)
88 Bartley Road
Flanders, NJ 07836
Telephone: (973) 252-9800
Fax: (973) 252-7171
E-Mail: tdi@gti.net
www.tdi-dog.org

TRAINING

Association of Pet Dog Trainers (APDT)
150 Executive Center Drive Box 35
Greenville, SC 29615
Telephone: (800) PET-DOGS
Fax: (864) 331-0767
E-Mail: information@apdt.com
www.apdt.com

International Association of Animal Behavior Consultants (IAABC)
565 Callery Road
Cranberry Township, PA 16066
E-Mail: info@iaabc.org
www.iaabc.org

National Association of Dog Obedience Instructors (NADOI)
PMB 369
729 Grapevine Hwy.
Hurst, TX 76054-2085
www.nadoi.org

VETERINARY AND HEALTH RESOURCES

Academy of Veterinary Homeopathy (AVH)
P.O. Box 9280
Wilmington, DE 19809
Telephone: (866) 652-1590
Fax: (866) 652-1590
www.theavh.org

American Academy of Veterinary Acupuncture (AAVA)
P.O. Box 1058
Glastonbury, CT 06033
Telephone: (860) 632-9911
Fax: (860) 659-8772
www.aava.org

American Animal Hospital Association (AAHA)
12575 W. Bayaud Ave.
Lakewood, CO 80228
Telephone: (303) 986-2800
Fax: (303) 986-1700
E-Mail: info@aahanet.org
www.aahanet.org/index.cfm

American College of Veterinary Internal Medicine (ACVIM)
1997 Wadsworth Blvd., Suite A
Lakewood, CO 80214-5293
Telephone: (800) 245-9081
Fax: (303) 231-0880
Email: ACVIM@ACVIM.org
www.acvim.org

American College of Veterinary Ophthalmologists (ACVO)
P.O. Box 1311
Meridian, ID 83860
Telephone: (208) 466-7624
Fax: (208) 466-7693
E-Mail: office09@acvo.com
www.acvo.com

American Holistic Veterinary Medical Association (AHVMA)
2218 Old Emmorton Road
Bel Air, MD 21015
Telephone: (410) 569-0795
Fax: (410) 569-2346
E-Mail: office@ahvma.org
www.ahvma.org

American Veterinary Medical Association (AVMA)
1931 North Meacham Road, Suite 100
Schaumburg, IL 60173-4360
Telephone: (847) 925-8070
Fax: (847) 925-1329
E-Mail: avmainfo@avma.org
www.avma.org

ASPCA Animal Poison Control Center
Telephone: (888) 426-4435
www.aspca.org

British Veterinary Association (BVA)
7 Mansfield Street
London
W1G 9NQ
Telephone: 0207 636 6541
Fax: 0207 908 6349
E-Mail: bvahq@bva.co.uk
www.bva.co.uk

Canine Eye Registration
Foundation (CERF)
VMDB/CERF
1717 Philo Rd
P O Box 3007
Urbana, IL 61803-3007
Telephone: (217) 693-4800
Fax: (217) 693-4801
E-Mail: CERF@vmbd.org
www.vmdb.org

Orthopedic Foundation for Animals (OFA)
2300 NE Nifong Blvd
Columbus, Missouri 65201-3856
Telephone: (573) 442-0418
Fax: (573) 875-5073
Email: ofa@offa.org
www.offa.org

US Food and Drug Administration Center for Veterinary Medicine (CVM)
7519 Standish Place
HFV-12
Rockville, MD 20855-0001
Telephone: (240) 276-9300 or (888) INFO-FDA
http://www.fda.gov/cvm

PUBLICATIONS
BOOKS
Anderson, Teoti. *The Super Simple Guide to Housetraining.* Neptune City: TFH Publications, 2004.

Anne, Jonna, with Mary Straus. *The Healthy Dog Cookbook: 50 Nutritious and Delicious Recipes Your Dog Will Love.* UK: Ivy Press Limited, 2008.

Bedwell-Wilson, Wendy. *Yorkshire Terriers.* Neptune City: TFH Publications, 2006.

Dainty, Suellen. *50 Games to Play With Your Dog.* UK: Ivy Press Limited, 2007.

Morgan, Diane. *Complete Guide to Dog Care.* Neptune City: TFH Publications, 2011.

Schimpf, Sheila. *Yorkshire Terrier.* Neptune City: TFH Publications, 2011.

Wood, Deborah. *Little Dogs.* Neptune City: TFH Publications, 2004.
—*The Yorkshire Terrier.* Neptune City: TFH Publications, 2005.

MAGAZINES
AKC Family Dog
American Kennel Club
260 Madison Avenue
New York, NY 10016
Telephone: (800) 490-5675
E-Mail: familydog@akc.org
www.akc.org/pubs/familydog

AKC Gazette
American Kennel Club
260 Madison Avenue
New York, NY 10016
Telephone: (800) 533-7323
E-Mail: gazette@akc.org
www.akc.org/pubs/gazette

Dog & Kennel
Pet Publishing, Inc.
7-L Dundas Circle
Greensboro, NC 27407
Telephone: (336) 292-4272
Fax: (336) 292-4272
E-Mail: info@petpublishing.com
www.dogandkennel.com

Dogs Monthly
Ascot House
High Street, Ascot,
Berkshire SL5 7JG
United Kingdom
Telephone: 0870 730 8433
Fax: 0870 730 8431
E-Mail: admin@rtc-associates.
freeserve.co.uk
www.corsini.co.uk/dogsmonthly

WEBSITES
Nylabone
www.nylabone.com

TFH Publications, Inc.
www.tfh.com

INDEX

Note: **Boldfaced** numbers indicate illustrations.

PHOTO CREDITS

ACKNOWLEDGMENTS

They say it takes a village to raise a child; I think the same is true of a book. There are quite a few who helped me, that's for sure.

First of all was my Yorkie Robbie. He was the household maître-d' for 15 years, keeper of the front door, and my shadow. Although he passed away in 1993, I still miss him.

But if Robbie was the inspiration, others gave more concrete help. Many members of the Yorkshire Terrier Club of America (YTCA) were generous of their time and sent in wonderful pictures and stories. I couldn't have done the grooming chapter without Barbara Beissel, and thanks go as well to Catherine Murphy, DVM, for side-checking the health chapter. I also must mention my mentor, Karen Huey, as much of the information in the training chapters originated with her. However, although the data stemmed in large part from others, any mistakes in *Yorkshire Terrier* lie only with me.

I hope you had as much fun reading this book as I did writing it.

ABOUT THE AUTHOR

Sandy Bergstrom Mesmer grew up in West Hartford, Connecticut. She attended her first dog show when she was eight and fell instantly in love with all of the different breeds and the atmosphere of knowledge and purpose—not to mention the faint odor of hairspray.

Fast-forward 16 years and Sandy bought her first dog, a Yorkshire Terrier named Robbie of Badhadlan. He was her constant buddy and companion and introduced her to the fun and challenge of showing dogs.

Professionally, Sandy trained as a pastoral counselor affiliated with the Church of Scientology. She founded Jefferson Academy, a private K through 8 school and was headmistress there for ten years. In 1994 she left the school and joined the Mace Kingsley Family Center, where she has worked ever since. She currently travels all over the world, working with families and their children.

Sandy began writing in 2000, publishing her first book, *How to Turn Your Dog into a Show-Off*, in 2002. She is also an acclaimed artist. Her training advice and artwork can be found at her website, www.about-small-dogs.com.

Sandy began breeding and showing Silky Terriers in 1981. Since then she has bred more than 85 champions, including several top winners. But her very first dog was Robbie. He was her best friend, house maître-d', and advisor for 15 years.

This book is dedicated to him.

ABOUT ANIMAL PLANET™

Animal Planet™ is the only television network dedicated exclusively to the connection between humans and animals. The network brings people of all ages together by tapping into our fundamental fascination with animals through an array of fresh programming that includes humor, competition, drama, and spectacle from the animal kingdom.

ABOUT *DOGS 101*

The most comprehensive—and most endearing—dog encyclopedia on television, *DOGS 101* spotlights the adorable, the feisty and the unexpected. A wide-ranging rundown of everyone's favorite dog breeds—from the Dalmatian to Xoloitzcuintli —this series surveys a variety of breeds for their behavioral quirks, genetic history, most famous examples and wildest trivia. Learn which dogs are best for urban living and which would be the best fit for your family. Using a mix of animal experts, pop-culture footage and stylized dog photography, *DOGS 101* is an unprecedented look at man's best friend.